NATIONAL TRUST HISTORIES
CAMBRIDGESHIRE
AND
MID ANGLIA

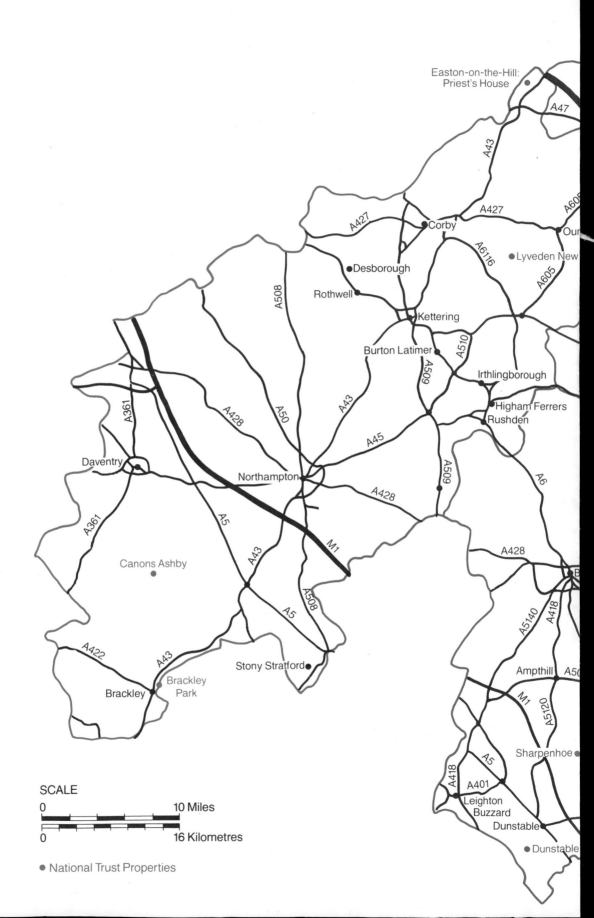

Easton-on-the-Hill:
Priest's House

A47

A43

A427

A427

A605

Corby

A6116

Lyveden New

Desborough

A605

Rothwell

A508

Kettering

A510

Burton Latimer

A509

Irthlingborough

A43

Higham Ferrers

A45

Rushden

Daventry

A428

A50

A509

A361

A428

Northampton

A6

A361

A5

A43

A428

Canons Ashby

A508

B

A5

A5140

A418

A422

A43

M1

Ampthill

A50

Brackley

Brackley
Park

Stony Stratford

M1

A5120

Sharpenhoe

A418

A5

A401

Leighton
Buzzard

Dunstable

Dunstable

SCALE

0   10 Miles

0   16 Kilometres

● National Trust Properties

NATIONAL TRUST HISTORIES
CAMBRIDGESHIRE
AND
MID ANGLIA
CHRISTOPHER TAYLOR

Series Editor Richard Muir

Willow Books
Collins
Grafton Street, London
in association with
The National Trust
1984

Willow Books
William Collins & Co Ltd
London Glasgow Sydney Auckland
Toronto Johannesburg

Taylor, Christopher
Cambridgeshire and mid Anglia.
(National Trust
regional history series)
1. Cambridgeshire – History
I. Title II. Series
942.6'5 DA670.C2

Hardback ISBN 0 00 218057 X
Paperback ISBN 0 00 218105 3

First published 1984
Copyright © 1984 Christopher Taylor and Lennard Books

Made by Lennard Books
Mackerye End, Harpenden,
Herts AL5 5DR

Editor Michael Leitch
Designed by David Pocknell's Company Ltd
Production Reynolds Clark Associates Ltd
Printed and bound in Spain by
TONSA, San Sebastian

Cover Photographs

Centre: Ely Cathedral

Top left: King's College, Cambridge

Top right: Earl's Barton Church

CONTENTS

EDITOR'S INTRODUCTION

Earlier in this century, geographers devoted much time to attempts to draw boundaries around geographical regions. Their failure reminds us of the impossibility of drawing sharp lines around areas which gradually merge into their neighbours. Our Mid Anglia comprises the new counties of Bedfordshire, Cambridgeshire and Northamptonshire. It does not proclaim its personality with great insistence, so that it is only when we realize that this region includes Northamptonshire, with the best assemblage of Saxon churches that any county can boast, the college buildings of Cambridge, and many fine post-medieval buildings such as Wimpole Hall and Kirby Hall that we begin to see it as a particularly fascinating part of England.

Geography and history provide several common denominators within the region. Rather than split Cambridgeshire in half we have included the Fens and Isle of Ely as part of Mid Anglia, while recognizing that their links with Cambridge are balanced by other strong ties with East Anglia, the subject of a future volume.

In the past as still today, Mid Anglia was a prosperous region with much valuable farmland. This prosperity helped to provide an exceptional legacy of fine stone churches and imposing houses. Most of the churches and houses still survive, along with a good legacy of vernacular buildings of a lower order. Sadly, much of the lovely, mature countryside in which these buildings stood has been lost to destructive modern farming methods. Some attractive countryside remains, and here the reader can discover the successive ages of farming which forged these rural vistas.

Christopher Taylor, the author, is a Principal Investigator for the Royal Commission on Historical Monuments and I doubt that anyone has ever known Mid Anglia as well as he does, for in the course of producing the various RCHM volumes on Cambridgeshire and Northamptonshire he explored every nook and cranny of those counties; he has also conducted many archaeological surveys in Bedfordshire. He has tutored and encouraged scores of archaeologists and amateur enthusiasts; taught me far more about the history of the landscape than any other expert, and it is interesting to see how his once-provocative ideas about the achievements and contributions of ancient and medieval people have now become part of mainstream archaeological thinking. Christopher Taylor is the author of several books on the history of our landscape, including volumes on Dorset and Cambridgeshire in the *Making of the English Landscape* series, *Roads and Tracks of Britain* and *Fields in the English Landscape,* while the fascinating results of his long research into the history and layout of English settlement were recently published in the highly praised *Village and Farmstead.*

Richard Muir
Great Shelford, 1983

ORIGINS

There is no familiar name attaching to that part of England which covers the modern counties of Bedfordshire, Cambridgeshire and Northamptonshire. The term Mid Anglia is perhaps reasonable, in that the ancient Saxon kingdom of the Middle Angles certainly included most of the region under discussion.

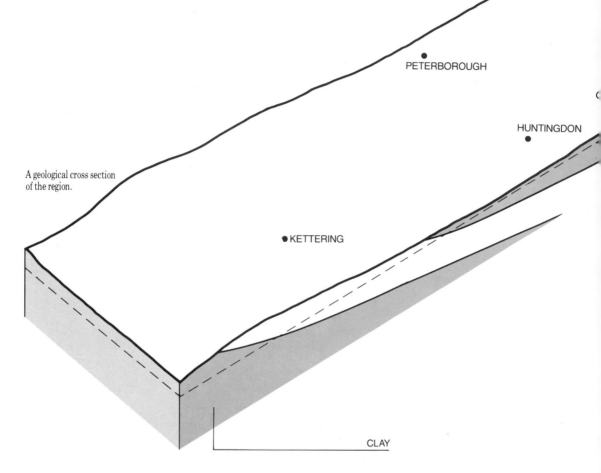

A geological cross section of the region.

PETERBOROUGH

HUNTINGDON

KETTERING

CLAY

The area is not the best-known part of England although Cambridge is a major tourist centre and Ely, with its beautiful cathedral, is also celebrated. There is no majestic scenery, no mountains, no roaring streams, but instead rolling hills, broad rivers and flat fenland. This is a region that is often traversed by visitors going elsewhere. Most of the main arteries of Britain, the A1, A5 and M1, and both East and West Coast main railway lines all cross it. The majority of its historic towns are now by-passed, and the main railway towns, such as Northampton, Bedford and Peterborough, hardly inspire the casual traveller to stop. Yet the region has much to offer both visitor and resident once their interest is aroused. Within it lies the richest farming land in England, where people have toiled for millennia to produce landscapes of considerable beauty and great interest.

The lack of high land and the gently undulating terrain are the results of geological events that took place in the very remote past, long before the appearance of man. All the underlying rocks in the area are relatively soft and easily worn away by rain and rivers. Chalk, clay, sandstone

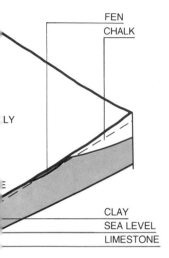

FEN
CHALK
LY
E
CLAY
SEA LEVEL
LIMESTONE

and tilting took place over a period of some sixty million years.

By about two million years ago, the general appearance of Mid Anglia had been fixed. Since then, two major processes have added the final details to the landscape. The first occurred in the Great Ice Age, or rather a whole series of Ice Ages, when the land was either covered by very thick sheets of ice or was torn apart by frost action and the work of huge rivers flowing in from the nearby ice. The result was a general smoothing and levelling of the soft rocks; the establishment of the great rivers of the Ouse and the Nene in their broad valleys, and, soon afterwards, the clothing of the landscape by vegetation.

The second was the formation of the Eastern Fens. The ice left behind a great basin in the east of Mid Anglia which became a battleground between the sea and the inland rivers whose waters met and mixed there. In the south of the fens, the rivers, though restrained by the sea, won the battle and their waters spread and created vast lagoons and marshes which became the peat fens. In the north, victory went to the sea which deposited great tracts of marine mud, now forming the northern silt fens. Eventually, the sea retreated and the land emerged as the great flat fenland expanses.

Although these fens are now largely cultivated farmland – indeed, the most valuable agricultural land in Britain – a few traces of the ancient undrained fens still endure. The best site to visit is Wicken Fen, north-east of Cambridge, which is in National Trust care. Here, not only the natural vegetation of flat fenland but also its myriad animal and bird life have been miraculously preserved and are now carefully managed to give a remarkable insight into the world before man.

An old Fenland wind pump re-erected and restored at Wicken Fen nature reserve.

and limestone predominate. All were laid down millions of years ago in the waters of shallow seas which then covered the region. Between each period of inundation by water the sea floor was uplifted and tilted slightly to the south-east. As a result, the whole area slopes in a general way from north-west to south-east; the oldest rocks lie in the west, and the youngest in the east. This process of deposition

An aerial view of the Fens near Chatteris showing modern fields and the branching patterns of former river courses.

A wide variety of local building materials is displayed in the vernacular architecture of the region. Above is Northamptonshire stone, near Wadenhoe.

Pargeting or decorative plaster work, Fen Ditton, Cambridgeshire.

Its complex geological history not only gives the region its overall shape, but also endows it with much of its character. For man has exploited nature's gifts and this is particularly well demonstrated in the case of the rocks. The splendid fine-grained limestones of the north and west have been cut and shaped to produce many of the exquisite great houses and churches both within the region and beyond. The more widely obtainable but coarser limestones form the basic structures of countless farmhouses and cottages in the same north-western quarter, while the specially 'fissile' limestone from localities such as Collyweston has been split to form the distinctive grey-blue 'slates' which cover the roofs of many Northamptonshire houses.

In the south and south-east, bands of hard chalk or 'clunch' have been quarried and used either as blocks to build cottages or farms or

Cambridge brick, near Horningsea, Cambridgeshire.

Clunch, near Horningsea, Cambridgeshire.

delicately carved to embellish many church interiors. In more recent times, the older clays have been dug and baked into bricks. These have produced, according to the composition and the methods of firing employed, both the soft red bricks so characteristic of parts of Bedfordshire and west Cambridgeshire, and the less attractive but widespread grey-white bricks of Cambridgeshire, the fens and fenland edges. The fens themselves, at least until the last century or so, have yielded the reeds to thatch the timber-framed buildings in Cambridgeshire, the wood coming from the trees which grow so well on the heavy clayland. Reeds for thatching are still harvested at Wicken Fen.

Flint, Babraham, Cambridgeshire.

Timber-framing, Elstow, Bedfordshire.

PREHISTORIC AND ROMAN TIMES

Mid Anglia is not remarkable for its obviously visible prehistoric and Roman remains. There are no clearly recognizable ancient tombs, relatively few hill-top forts and no well-preserved great Roman villas to see. This lack of prehistoric and Roman monuments is usually interpreted as meaning that few, if any, prehistoric or Romano-British communities lived in Mid Anglia and that it remained a dark and forested countryside until the arrival of the Saxons. Nothing could be further from the truth.

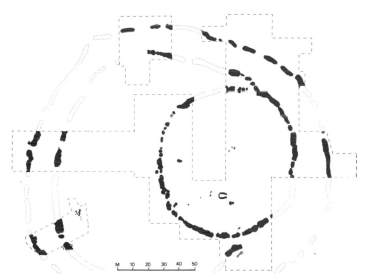

Prehistoric and Roman people lived here in their thousands, settling in countless villages and farmsteads, cutting down the primeval forests and cultivating tens of thousands of acres of fields. The reason why so little of this activity still remains to be seen is because, in this rich and prosperous land, successive communities have also lived and farmed. As a result they have removed almost all the obvious remains of earlier occupations.

Yet archaeologists, working all over Mid Anglia, have found, by excavation and aerial photography, evidence that most of the region was totally settled and exploited by man

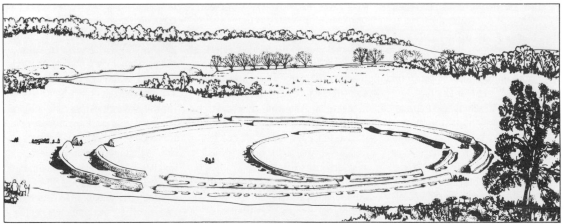

A drawn reconstruction of the Neolithic causewayed enclosure at Briar Hill, near Northampton.

for several millennia before the Saxons arrived. The handful of visible prehistoric and Roman archaeological sites in Mid Anglia, fascinating though many of them may be, are only a tiny fragment of what once existed.

There are no obvious antiquities to testify to the greater part of man's tenancy of Mid Anglia. From around 10000 to 5000 BC, the whole region was occupied by small groups of 'Mesolithic' or Middle Stone Age hunters and gatherers eking out a living in the forest and along the rivers. Nothing much remains of these people except minute scraps of expertly worked flints or 'microliths' which were their flint tools. Then, around 5000 BC, new ideas, and perhaps new people, arrived here.

Suddenly the population rose, farming and forest clearance began. Tens of thousands of acres of primeval woodland were removed and replaced by fields and pastureland. The outlines of these fields have long since been destroyed, but some of the pastures still survive. The grassland of Dunstable Downs, Bedfordshire, part of the National Trust's holding in that county, and Newmarket Heath in south-east Cambridgeshire were given their present appearance by the farmers of 5000 – 4000 BC. It was they, or rather their sheep and cattle, who produced the close-cropped downland. Yet some indication that they formed themselves into a complex and highly developed society can be seen at two remaining monuments of this period, both in south Bedfordshire.

One is Waluds Bank, a low horseshoe-shaped rampart set around the source of the River Lea that emerges from the chalk just north of Leagrave Railway Station on the northern outskirts of Luton. The other is Maiden Bower which is situated on the downland west of Dunstable and now sadly almost destroyed by a quarry. There remain the defensive ramparts of a small Iron Age fort, and under it, as excavations have proved, a

Top: Crop marks in fields near Maxey Church, Cambridgeshire, reveal ancient enclosures, ditches and habitations of several ages.
Above: An aerial view showing the ramparts of Borough Hill fort.

Neolithic 'camp' bounded by a series of banks and ditches interrupted by gaps or causeways. Neither of these is in any way defensive, and their real purpose was probably as the communal and commercial foci for the areas around them. They can thus be seen as rallying points, trading places or tribal meeting places for the many thousands of people who lived in the region. And while these are the only two such sites now visible, others such as those at Cardington, near Bedford, as well as major Neolithic villages which existed near Northampton and burial-places close to Thrapston, also in Northamptonshire, all indicate that by at least 3000 BC Mid Anglia

supported a well-populated and organized countryside.

As the centuries rolled by, people acquired the use of copper and bronze to make their tools. Bronze Age people lived in Mid Anglia between 2000 and 650 BC. During this time the population continued to rise and farmsteads and villages were scattered almost everywhere except in the wet fenlands. Archaeologists have not only found traces of these people throughout Mid Anglia, they have also proved that much of the primeval woodland was removed by them. By the end of the Bronze Age, there was certainly less woodland to be seen than there is today and more people lived there than did in early medieval

Landscaped beechwoods planted at the Iron Age hill fort of Wandlebury in Cambridgeshire, now enclosed in an attractive nature reserve.

farmsteads and villages in every part of the region. Even on the heaviest clayland which in later times (and in places even today) was dominated by forest, Iron Age farmers established their homes and farms. Indeed, within the ancient medieval forest of Salcey, in south-east Northamptonshire, near the village of Hartwell, still protected amongst the Forestry Commission's conifer plantations, are the remains of a small Iron Age farm. It is now called the 'Egg Ring', because it consists of an oval bank and ditch enclosing about two acres. This site vividly illustrates the extent to which Mid Anglia was overcrowded at the end of prehistoric times, for it shows that even the heaviest, least tractable soils, were worked.

Two important developments followed from this overcrowding. One was that every part of the region was exploited and thus it had to be divided and marked out by boundaries which variously separated farms, villages and tribal territories. Many of these boundaries are known but now are only visible from the air. A rare survival is the triple bank and ditch system which runs along the road from the village of Stowe-Nine-Churches, westwards towards Farthingstone, in Northamptonshire.

The other result of overcrowding was almost continuous warfare, as the Iron Age people struggled to control land, wealth and power. Hill forts were constructed, their interiors defended by massive banks and ditches, each being the focus of a tribal or sub-tribal area. From these places kings or chieftains may have ruled, and to them people from the surrounding areas fled at times of danger. Other forts were permanently occupied as major administrative centres. There are a number of such forts in Mid Anglia. One of the best, and certainly by far the largest, is that at Borough Hill, near Daventry in Northamptonshire. Though most of this area is inaccessible, being occupied by a

times. Even so, it is still difficult now to see many places that were created by these people. Many of our present-day villages lie on top of their villages and our fields have destroyed their fields. All that survive – and then only in a few places – are some of the burial mounds of this period.

The best example of these burial mounds is the small group known as the Five Knolls, on Dunstable Downs. Other isolated mounds can be seen all along the chalklands of south Cambridgeshire, often marked as 'Tumuli' on Ordnance Survey maps, but even these are the last surviving remnants of what were once considerable cemeteries. Bronze Age people also

lived, and buried their dead, in places far from the dry chalklands, as can be seen by the line of three burial mounds which stand on a hill overlooking the River Nene at Woodford, near Thrapston in Northamptonshire. These, known as The Three Hills, lie as they always have done, surrounded by arable land, and now accessible to the modern explorer by a short if muddy track.

In the closing centuries of the prehistoric era, bronze was replaced by iron as the main material for tools. In the Iron Age, Mid Anglia seems to have been threatened by over-population. Archaeologists have found traces of hundreds of Iron Age

BBC transmitting station, its northern third, where the massive ramparts and entrances are best preserved, is a public open space. Other Iron Age fortresses easy of access include Hunsbury, just south of Northampton and now part of a country park, and Wandlebury, immediately south-east of Cambridge, situated amongst lovely landscaped beechwoods and now serving as a nature reserve. There are two small fortresses east of Sandy in Bedfordshire, one of which lies in grounds maintained by the Royal Society for the Protection of Birds.

The Impact of Rome

In AD 43 Mid Anglia like the rest of southern England was conquered by the Roman army and passed into the Roman Empire for almost four hundred years. The effects of Roman administration and ideas were immense. The immediate results were the end of all internal fighting, the establishment of peace and the development of commerce which included a lively export trade. All these factors allowed the population to increase yet again, which in turn produced an even more intensive agriculture. Farmsteads and villages now multiplied, many standing as little as five hundred yards apart. All these sites have now been destroyed and can be discovered only by excavation or aerial photography.

One particularly important expansion was into the silt fenlands of north Cambridgeshire and around the fen edges, in places where it had been impossible for man to live in the pre-Roman Iron Age. As a consequence of slightly drier conditions brought about by a lowering of the sea level, together with massive drainage works which only the Romans with their organization and engineering skills could undertake, thousands of new villages appeared in and around the fens. Few of these now exist, most having been totally destroyed by ploughing as modern farmers

A section of the Roman Car Dyke canal survives near Landbeach in Cambridgeshire.

exploited the same rich fenland. However, one or two survive, perhaps the most notable being at Denney, near Waterbeach, north of Cambridge. There, in the care of the Department of the Environment, is the remarkable structure belonging to the medieval abbey. In the surrounding land there are low banks and depressions marking the monastic fish ponds and yards. But these banks are not entirely monastic. The monastic features were fitted into a much older arrangement of ditches which bounded the fields and part of the settlement area of a very large Roman village which once occupied the site. Such ditches, visually unimpressive

Now a country lane – the Roman road near Wandlebury hill fort.

than the modern village. Fragments of the walls of this villa still stand and are incorporated in modern walls on the north side of Church Hill and the south-west side of the Rectory garden at Castor.

Perhaps the greatest impact of the Roman Empire was that it gave Mid Anglia its first towns and its first constructed roads. Many of the modern towns of the area had their origins as Roman urban centres. Cambridge is one, though Roman Cambridge was built to the north of the River Cam in the area known as Castle Hill and not on the low-lying land to the south where the present town centre lies. The core of the Roman town of Cambridge is now occupied by the offices of the County Council, whose members and officers probably control and direct the same area of land and its people that its Roman predecessors did. Towcester – as part of its name, from *castra* or 'camp', suggests – is another Roman town. Here the roughly rectangular shape of the old centre still reflects the pattern imposed by the Roman walls, though these have now gone. Godmanchester, in Cambridgeshire, is yet another, while Peterborough, Oundle, Thrapston, Kettering and Higham Ferrers all had very large Roman settlements of town-like proportions near to them.

Of the great Roman roads, many still remain as major through routes. A length of Watling Street, now the A5, crosses western Bedfordshire and bisects Northamptonshire, while the straight sections of the A604 Cambridge – Huntingdon road and the A1 between Alconbury Hill and Chesterton are visual expressions of the impact of the Roman road engineer. Other Roman roads have fallen into disuse and make attractive walks for any visitor to Mid Anglia. The old Roman road between Colchester and Cambridge now survives as a wonderful chain of green lanes extending south-east from Wandlebury near Cambridge as far as Horseheath.

though they are, are a rare survival in the modern landscape and give us a vivid reminder of the almost total exploitation of the countryside of Mid Anglia in Roman times.

Along with the countless new Roman villages and farmsteads, there appeared great Roman houses, usually known as villas. Their remains have been discovered all over Mid Anglia, with major concentrations to the west of Peterborough and around Towcester in Northamptonshire. The largest of these villas, perhaps the largest in Britain, lay under what is now the village of Castor, near Peterborough, and covered an area more extensive

THE COMING OF THE SAXONS

If the landscape outlines of Mid Anglia had been drawn by the end of the fourth century AD, the next six hundred years or so, when the area was under the control of the Saxons, saw the framework of the modern landscape firmly established. Yet the Saxon invaders did not import from the continent everything that historians have in the past suggested. For instance, the villages which dot the landscape are not Saxon at all, or at least only a few are, and even they are of a very late Saxon date. For, when the Saxons came into Mid Anglia in the early fifth century, they were faced not with an empty or sparsely populated countryside, but one which was full to overflowing with Roman villages and farmsteads.

The Saxons could not kill or drive out thousands of native Britons, so their leaders gradually took political control and slowly absorbed the Britons into their culture. More importantly, when the Saxons came to seek places to live, there were few empty spots where they might establish their homes. Therefore they either took over the existing Roman villages or farmsteads or set up new ones in the few vacant places that remained.

Archaeologists have found the evidence for this in recent years, especially in Bedfordshire and Northamptonshire where it has been shown that, far from living in the villages that now exist, the early Saxons lived in small hamlets and farmsteads scattered across the countryside or they rebuilt the older Roman villages. Nor, apparently, did

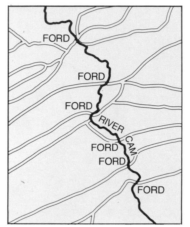
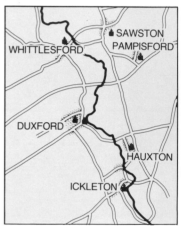

The ancient Icknield Way trackway influenced the growth of Saxon and medieval villages in the area south of Cambridge. Several appeared where the tracks crossed the River Cam.

The Icknield Way survives as a village street in Duxford.

the Saxons introduce the open-field system into Mid Anglia, as has often been assumed. It would not have been possible even if they had wished to do so, for the land was already very neatly divided up into countless Roman fields. What they actually did was to use the existing fields, which they then gradually modified over the centuries until they became open strip fields of the kind described in so many school books.

The modern villages of Mid Anglia evolved gradually over a long period of time, often as a result of forces which we do not yet fully understand. One way in which a large number of villages developed was through the growing together of groups of closely set Saxon or Roman farmsteads and hamlets as people abandoned other settlements and concentrated in one place. Just why this took place is not yet known, but it seems to have occurred almost spontaneously as late as the eighth or ninth century AD, long after the Saxons had first arrived.

Many villages in Mid Anglia show this development in their present layout. These are the villages which seem delightfully formless, with no one clear centre and with winding streets which meet and divide or open into tiny greens. Newnham, south of Daventry in Northamptonshire, is a particularly good example, as is nearby Badby. In southern Cambridgeshire, Duxford, which has two churches marking the positions of the two earlier settlement centres, and Meldreth, which is strung out along a winding road for nearly two miles, are both instances of this type of 'polyfocal' or several-centred village.

On the other hand, many villages in the region can be shown actually to have been the result of deliberate planning in late Saxon times, perhaps in the tenth, eleventh or later centuries. What appears to have happened was that many of the great landowning lords, probably motivated by economic reasons, planned new villages or replanned old

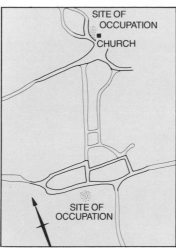
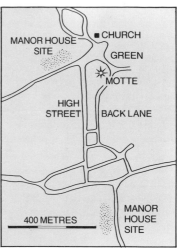

The polyfocal village of Wollaston in Northamptonshire has more than one village nucleus; two separate sites were settled in Saxon times.

The small green beside the church at Wollaston.

settlements, while at the same time reorganizing the field systems around them. Many villages show that they were planned in this way, though it is not always easy to recognize them, for later changes have often modified or obscured the original neatly planned layout. Thriplow in south Cambridgeshire, with a somewhat distorted 'grid pattern' of streets, is one such village, as is Spratton, north of Northampton, and Flore to the west of Northampton. Other villages with neat rectangular or triangular greens such as Eltisley in Cambridgeshire and Creaton in Northamptonshire were also probably laid out in Saxon times as new, regularly planned villages.

It was during the first part of the Saxon period that Mid Anglia achieved a brief independence. The Mid Angles seemed to have been a loose confederation of tribes with no single king or overlord and in the end this lack of cohesion was to be their downfall. By the middle of the seventh century Mid Anglia had been absorbed into the powerful kingdom of Mercia to the west.

Mercia continued to expand eastwards and, on the eastern borders of Cambridgeshire, met the kingdom of East Anglia. East Anglia was far less powerful than Mercia, but the western boundary was occupied mainly by fenland. Only in south-east Cambridgeshire was there direct and easy access between the two. And at this very place there remains a series of great defensive ditches, the Devil's Dyke, the Fleam Dyke, the Brent Ditch and the Heydon Dyke. The last two are now either fragmentary or largely destroyed, but the Fleam Dyke and the Devil's Dyke both extend for miles across the chalk downland, effectively blocking access into East Anglia. Although the date of their construction is not known, it is likely that these dykes are the remains of a fluctuating boundary between the two Saxon kingdoms in the late seventh or early eighth century. Both the Fleam and the Devil's Dykes now not only stand as evocative reminders of the inter-tribal wars which finally led to the establishment of England as a nation, they also provide easy access via their modern rampart-top footpaths to a rich variety of natural history preserved on their grassy banks and within their ditches.

The Devil's Dyke, Cambridgeshire, part of a mighty defensive system which probably defined the boundary between Mercia and East Anglia.

Early Towns and Churches

The late Saxon period saw the revival of two features of the Mid Anglian landscape: towns and churches. The old Roman towns of the area were partly or completely abandoned in early Saxon times and lost their commercial and administrative functions. Towards the end of Saxon times, in the eighth, ninth and tenth centuries, new towns appeared. These were, at least in part, the creations of the Danish invaders who had occupied the northern part of Mid Anglia by the end of the ninth century. The Danes not only created fortresses to control their conquests, but, contrary to popular legend, were prodigious traders and so required trading centres. As a result the Danes built a whole series of fortified towns or 'burghs' which combined both functions. In Mid Anglia both Cambridge and Huntingdon were founded by the Danes and both still

retain the traces of these original towns. At Cambridge, the straight Bridge Street leading down to the River Cam at Magdalene Bridge, where the riverside quays lay, was the main thoroughfare of Danish Cambridge. The much-rebuilt St Clement's Church half-way along the street tells us by its very name that we are in a Danish town, for St Clement was a favourite church dedication for Christianized Danes.

Other towns were created by the English kings, again partly for administrative and commercial purposes, but also because they too required fortresses to protect their domains. The old Roman town of Towcester was refortified and given a new life in 917 by King Edward the Elder. More impressive was the foundation of Bedford, also by King Edward, in 915–16. Despite the destruction wrought by development

in the modern town, the basic grid pattern of the streets, laid out in late Saxon times, still survives.

Visually more attractive are the early churches of Mid Anglia. Christianity came to the area in the seventh century but little or nothing remains of the very first churches, which were probably built of timber. By the eighth century the first stone churches appeared and these gradually increased in number over the next two or three hundred years. However, these churches did not appear in the landscape in a haphazard fashion. Their arrival came about through a complex pattern of ecclesiastical administration which had evolved by late Saxon times, and because piety was increasingly taken up by the local lords. The first churches were built to carry out two distinct functions. Some were established as parts of monastic

The remarkable Saxon tower of Brigstock Church, Northamptonshire. The tower shows that a church existed here when Brigstock was the centre of a great royal estate.

houses, such as Ely founded in 673, Peterborough founded in about 650, Ramsey about 969 and Thorney about 670. Nothing remains at any of these places of the first structures.

More important were the churches built to serve the ordinary people. The earliest of these were not the familiar parish churches but the so-called 'minster' churches. These were placed in the centres of large estates, or at important administrative centres, and were run not by a single priest, but by a group of clerics. These clerics held services at the church and also travelled through the surrounding area preaching to the people either in the open air or in temporary wooden chapels. A number of minster churches are known, but few have traces of Saxon work within them, having been rebuilt many times. One such is Fawsley Church, which now stands quite alone in the magnificent parkland of Fawsley Hall, south of Daventry in Northamptonshire. Its solitary position and the fact that it has nothing in its structure dating before the thirteenth century make it hard to believe that it was once the minster church of a royal Saxon estate which covered most of north-west Northamptonshire, and that it stood in the centre of a flourishing village. Later events have worked to produce its present delightful appearance; much more important is its status as the major centre of early Christianity in the county.

Several other churches known to have been early minsters also have no physical remains from the early period. King's Cliffe, also in Northamptonshire, is one, though its great size suggests that it was always important. Horningsea, just east of Cambridge, is another, and there a few fragments of the early church do indeed survive. However, the churches at Maulden in Bedfordshire and King's Sutton in south-west Northamptonshire, both early minsters, have, like Fawsley, no indication of their great antiquity. On the other hand, some of these minster churches do have significant remains. Brigstock, in Northamptonshire, which appears to have been at the centre of another royal estate, still has its original late Saxon tower with a semi-circular stair turret attached to it. It is clear that this tower is all that remains of a very large Saxon church. Much more complete is Great Paxton Church in Cambridgeshire. Though externally it appears of later medieval date, no visitor should be put off by this. Inside it contains the greater part of a cruciform and aisled late Saxon structure built on a grandiose scale.

Yet though Great Paxton is impressive, it is quite outshone by Brixworth, in Northamptonshire. Here is a building which has been described as 'perhaps the most important architectural memorial of the seventh century surviving north of the Alps'. It was founded in 675, as a minster, by the then Abbot of Peterborough. Despite inevitably being much altered in the succeeding centuries, it remains the greatest Saxon building in England and is almost cathedral-like in its proportions. It is now shorn of its original aisles, though the blocked-up arches remain, built of Roman bricks which must have come from an unknown Roman building near at hand. Roman bricks and tiles also occur elsewhere in the structure. Brixworth, in its size and sophisticated arrangement, shows well the greatest achievement of the Saxon church builders.

As time went by, many of the villages originally served by minster churches acquired their own parish churches. These were erected largely by local lords. Over most of Mid Anglia it was not until the twelfth century that most villages had churches, for the process was a gradual one. Of the late Saxon parish churches, few survive except as mere fragments. The lower parts of the tower at Clapham, in Bedfordshire, are, with the tower at Earls Barton, east of Northampton, all that remain of any great structure.

The church of Earls Barton stands on the edge of a low spur, overlooking the village. Behind it, and protecting it from attackers approaching across the level land from the north, is a gigantic bank and ditch. This is perhaps prehistoric in origin, but it was probably refurbished in late Saxon times to defend the area behind it which includes the church. This area was presumably the fortified homestead of a late Saxon lord who built his church there. Yet the church was not, so it seems, a minster church. The tower that survives, decorated with curious flat bands of stone which possibly echo earlier timber construction, may have been a tiny nave with rooms above it. The high external doorways indicate that the upper floors have some special purpose, and certainly the tower had only a small chancel attached to it. The best explanation is that the tower itself was the lord's residence, as well as being the church's nave.

Above: Detail of the impressive late Saxon interior at Great Paxton Church, Cambridgeshire. **Below:** Brixworth Church, Northamptonshire, possibly the most complete and certainly the most impressive of all Saxon churches in England.

The late Saxon tower of Earls Barton Church, Northamptonshire, which was probably built as a combined nave and lordly residence.

THE FIXING OF THE LANDSCAPE

The centuries between the arrival of William the Conqueror in 1066 and the accession of Elizabeth I saw the fixing of the landscape of Mid Anglia. At this time, the landscape was in a continual state of flux caused by drastic changes in population, the desires and aims of local lords, the appearance of commercially minded individuals, national and even international fluctuations in economic affairs, changes in religious attitudes and alterations in the climate.

The early part of the medieval period, between 1066 and around 1300, was one of rising population and economic expansion. The results of these general trends were most marked in the villages and other settlements in the Mid Anglian countryside. Many new villages appeared, founded by local lords who sought to exploit the value that lay in controlling a large mass of peasants who could be drafted into the new settlements and either pay rents or carry out services in return.

Existing villages grew larger to accommodate the increasing number of people, and they also became much more compact. A splendid example of this is Burwell in Cambridgeshire. The village is now an extremely large one, extending for almost two miles. But in the early twelfth century it was less than half this length, largely confined to a single main street. With the rising population, the village expanded northwards and developed an entirely new section which was laid out on top of the older fields of late Saxon Burwell.

It was at this time that some, but not all, of our villages took on something resembling their present form – and not in earlier Saxon times, as is so often supposed. It is interesting, too, that many of them changed their form and even their

sites. The reasons for such alterations are complex and not fully understood in every case, nevertheless a few of those which have been examined in detail are worth considering to indicate the forces at work.

Old Weston, in Cambridgeshire, is an instance of one type of movement. The village now lies on the northern side of a shallow valley, but its parish church stands alone on the opposite side of the valley. Archaeological work has shown that, in the eighth century, Old Weston lay around the church. In the following three hundred years it gradually moved down the hillside towards the stream, where the deeply cut hollow-ways of its former streets still survive. Then, quite suddenly, it was moved to its present site and given the neat single street with houses on both sides. This move must have been carried out by the local lord, though why it was done is not clear.

A better understood movement is that of Caxton, also in Cambridgeshire. There too the parish church is now quite isolated from the village which is situated on the A14, once the great medieval North Road and even earlier the Roman Ermine Street. There is no doubt that Caxton once lay round the church, for again old hollow-ways, once streets, still survive there and large quantities of pottery and other occupation débris

have been found. The move of the village to the main road was carried out in 1247 by the then lord, Baldwin de Freville. Here we can see why this was done. De Freville intended to make money by establishing a market situated on the main road and to this end he not only received a grant from the King to hold one, but also built the market place in the centre of the new village. This market place still exists though now it is a private garden.

Other lords laid out new planned extensions to their villages which they then sometimes sub-let to lesser lords. At Cottenham, in Cambridgeshire, the 'olde-worlde' green at the southern end of the village is not an ancient Saxon open space but part of a whole new addition to the older village centre to the north, laid out by the Bishops of Ely in the twelfth century and then let.

At Stoke Albany in the north of Northamptonshire, the village has two completely separate parts. The late Saxon Stoke Albany lay, as it still does, round a small green adjacent to the parish church at the foot of the slope. In the thirteenth century, the then lord, William de Albini, from whom the village takes part of its name, laid out a new settlement consisting of four parallel streets, together with a new manor house, on the hillside above. This planned hamlet, with the rebuilt fourteenth-century manor house, remains to this day.

These villages are all examples of lordly influence and power. But numerous other places changed in response to external events. Most notable of these were alterations in communications. As trade developed, towns appeared and flourished and some roads became important while others remained little used or were even abandoned. Villages on the new main roads flourished while others away from them slumbered on untouched. Caxton, noted above, was a village which was actually moved because of the potential of a main road. Other villages tended to drift slowly towards such roads. Stilton, in Cambridgeshire, later to become famous as a cheese market, actually once lay a little to the west of the old Roman road (now the A1). But it gradually expanded and moved towards the road and then extended along it. Even though the village is now by-passed, its continued importance as a stopping place on the Great North Road is still marked today, principally by the magnificent Bell Inn built of honey-coloured limestone and dated 1642.

A village which changed its position because of changes of communications of a lower order is Knapwell in Cambridgeshire. In the twelfth century the village lay along an east-to-west street with the parish church in the centre. In 1143 a small temporary castle was built at its eastern end where the street reached a ford, and its site is still marked by a grassy circular mound. But apart from one modern house and the church, nothing remains of the village, though the sites of the former houses, now low banks and scarps, lie in the paddocks on either side of the old street. The village actually lies some distance away along a north-to-south street. What happened at Knapwell was that, in the twelfth century and perhaps for long before, the east-to-west street was along the

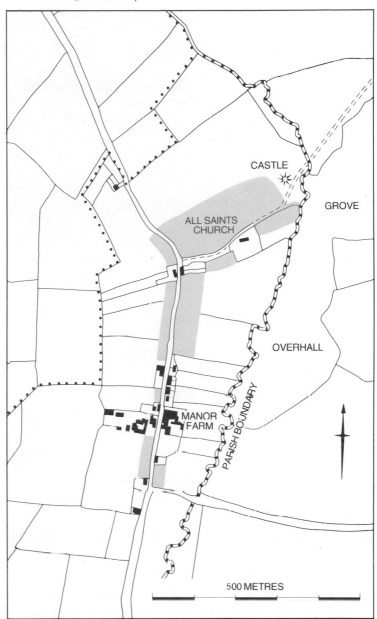

Knapwell, Cambridgeshire, where the village gradually turned from being arranged along an east-west road to one running north-south. Subsequently the village shrank in size leaving many empty spaces between the existing houses.

line of one of the main roads of the area. This road gradually fell out of use as long-distance traffic became concentrated on the old Roman road (now the A604) to the north and the ridge-way road (A45) to the south. It gradually became more convenient for the villagers at Knapwell to use the south line between the two main roads and as a result this grew in

importance. More significantly this road also led into the fields of Knapwell and so gradually the village turned itself through 90 degrees and occupied a new position. The process took many centuries and in fact was not finally completed until the eighteenth century.

Although the villages described here are good examples of

their kind, they must not be thought of as unusual. Most villages in Mid Anglia show the same kind of features if looked at with care. The most important point for both the interested visitor or resident is to realize that what they see today in the villages of the area are the results of profound change in both medieval times and later. We must not think that we are looking at the unaltered patterns of the remote past.

From the early fourteenth century Europe as a whole began to suffer from severe economic difficulties, of a kind which we are only too familiar with today. The result was a decline in prosperity, a halt to rising populations and the arrival of difficult times. These problems were accelerated into disaster when, in 1348–49, the Black Death struck. Within two years, perhaps one-third of the people of Mid Anglia were dead. The result of this was appalling for the survivors, but it also changed the face of our region out of all recognition. Yet the

changes, in the long term, were only indirectly related to the Black Death itself; many other factors were involved.

Certainly the massive reduction of population meant that several villages were wiped out and many more shrank away to a few houses. But then, with only a very few exceptions, within a few years the population began to rise again and the villages were re-established. The actual number of Mid Anglian villages that were deserted for ever because of the Black Death was relatively small. For example, in Northamptonshire, of the four hundred or so medieval villages there, only one, at Hale, near Apethorpe, was emptied of its inhabitants and never resettled. Yet the Black Death did have its profound effects. It seriously weakened many of the villages with the result that they were unable to survive later pressures that were imposed, and they then collapsed and vanished from the landscape.

Some villages lingered for

years before they were finally abandoned completely, but others fell prey to events which occurred in the century after the Black Death. One of the most significant of these in Mid Anglia was the growth of sheep farming consequent upon the late medieval woollen industry. The demand for large quantities of wool, combined with the reduced market for cereals and other crops, meant that it was in the commercial interests of large landowners and their major tenants to change the land from arable to pasture. This resulted in turn in a reduction in the agricultural labour force and many people were thrown out of work. In those places where villages had already been much reduced in size as a result of the economic decline of the early fourteenth century, and more particularly by the Black Death, it was relatively easy for the lords to remove the remaining inhabitants and create vast sheep pastures on the old fields.

During the fifteenth and

The great house and parish church at Fawsley, Northamptonshire, alone in the parkland laid out by Capability Brown, are redolent of eighteenth-century England. They stand as they do because two villages on the site were removed in the fifteenth century.

early sixteenth centuries, dozens of villages, particularly in Northamptonshire, finally disappeared in this way. Now only the grassy mounds of former houses, the hollow-ways that were once streets, and low banks formerly the old gardens, usually survive, with sometimes an isolated parish church. The most evocative is perhaps Fawsley, in Northamptonshire, where the parish church (mentioned earlier) stands completely alone in the parkland some distance from the great hall. It is perhaps difficult to imagine that in the middle of the fourteenth century there were two flourishing villages there, one round the church and the other south of the hall. Both were removed during the early fifteenth century by Richard Knightley, who carried out a deliberate policy of eviction immediately after he had bought the estate in 1415. Within a few years both villages had gone and sheep grazed on their sites.

Another village which was also removed at this time was Canons Ashby, not far from Fawsley. The desertion there occurred in the late fifteenth century, long before the magnificent house, now in the hands of the National Trust, was erected; it was carried out by the Prior of Canons Ashby. The priory itself lay round the now-abandoned parish church which was in fact the priory church, and the village lay to the north of it, along the road to Preston Capes. In 1489 the then Prior began a process of destruction when he pulled down three houses, and a few years later he evicted 24 people. By the end of the century the village had gone and the priory had its great sheep pastures. Ironically, in 1536 the priory itself was dissolved and the land of the village was incorporated into the gardens and park of the new house. An old hollow-way, banks and ditches marking the former houses and gardens of the village, still remain in the fields to the north-east of Canons Ashby House.

This scenario, in which the site of a village once cleared for sheep now lies within the parkland of a later great country house, is relatively common in Mid Anglia. It is ironic that such parks and houses would not exist today if the rapacious medieval lords had not removed their villages. Certainly Althorp House and its park, in Northamptonshire, were only created by the Spencer family long after the previous owners, the Catesbys, had ruthlessly destroyed the old village of Althorp in the fifteenth century (though the Spencers themselves were amongst the most notorious of village wreckers). Likewise, at Boughton, also in Northamptonshire, the magnificent park created by the Montagu family was only laid out because predecessors had destroyed Boughton village in the early fifteenth century. Slight traces of the old village of Boughton may still be seen in the parkland immediately north-east of the house.

Not all deserted medieval villages, however, lie in later parkland. Many remain tucked away

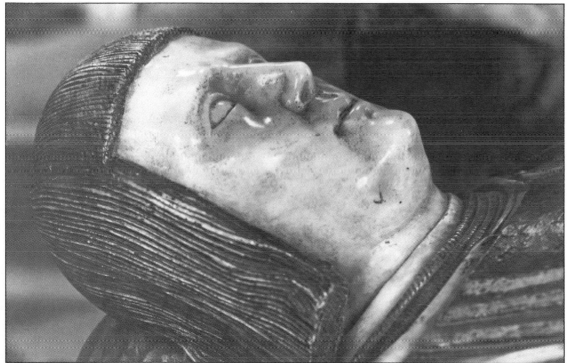

Sir Richard Knightley, died 1534, who lies with his wife and other members of his family in Fawsley Church, Northamptonshire. Over a period of five hundred years this family changed Fawsley from a typical rural parish with villages and fields to a glorious parkland and great house.

in the remote corners of our region waiting to surprise the interested explorer. In Bedfordshire, the remains of the village of Chellington lie around the isolated and abandoned parish church, high on a hill above the River Ouse. The public footpath to Harrold still follows the hollowed line of the main street. Similarly the bridleway from Braunston in north-west Northamptonshire which runs across the River Leam to Wolfhamcote, in Warwickshire, skirts the abandoned village of Braunstonbury, whose moated manor house, former streets and houses may still be recognized. In Cambridgeshire, the former village of Clopton, which has two moated manor-house sites as well as the remains of great fish ponds, and which was removed for sheep by John Fisher, a rich London merchant, in 1495, can still be seen on the hillside west of the present village of Croydon. The footpath from Croydon to Tadlow crosses the site.

The greatly increased population of early medieval times was not all housed in villages. In parts of Mid Anglia, where in the twelfth and thirteenth centuries there were still considerable areas of woodland or under-used arable land, many people established new hamlets or isolated farmsteads. This is especially true of south-east Cambridgeshire and large parts of north-east and south-west Bedfordshire. In these places, as well as the more typical villages, one finds that the winding lanes are punctuated by small groups of farmsteads rather like beads on a string. Many of these farmsteads are of seventeenth- and eighteenth-century date, but they occupy sites which are much older and which are the result of the colonization of the wastes and woodland by the burgeoning population of the twelfth and thirteenth centuries. These places often have names with 'end' or 'green' in them, such as Carlton Green in Cambridgeshire or Cross End in Bedfordshire.

The now ruinous church of Chellington, Bedfordshire, has only been abandoned as a place of worship

this century; but the village that once surrounded it vanished in the fifteenth century.

A typical example may be seen at Thurleigh, in north Bedfordshire. There the old compact village of Thurleigh lies in the bottom of a shallow valley, together with its church and the remains of its medieval castle. Along the winding road south to Ravensden is a whole line of farmsteads at 400-yard intervals, collectively called Scald End. Most are delightful seventeenth-century white-painted timber-framed structures, but all were first established in the thirteenth century, along with others long vanished. Indeed, at Scald End it has been shown that the ravages of the Black Death and other factors had their effects: archaeologists have found the traces of a number of other former houses and farmsteads which once stood between the existing farmsteads. Most of them were apparently abandoned towards the end of the fourteenth century, perhaps as a result of the Black Death, while others survived only to be deserted in the sixteenth and seventeenth centuries.

One characteristic feature of these former wooded areas is the number of 'moats' that exist within them. The Ordnance Survey maps of eastern Bedfordshire, western Cambridgeshire and south-eastern Cambridgeshire are dotted by moats. These are usually broad deep water-filled ditches which surround a rectangular island. There may still be a modern farmhouse within them, as at Manor Farm, Eltisley, Cambridgeshire, but more usually they lie empty, abandoned and uninviting, buried in old woodland or in remote corners of parishes and usually difficult of access. Not all moats, of course, lie in these old woodland areas, nor are they confined to out-of-the-way places. There is a general scatter of moated sites across Mid Anglia, though they tend to be fewer in Northamptonshire. They also occur widely within villages, often enclosing a 'manor farm'.

What were these moats? They are usually said to be small defensive works, but any visitor to one will soon see that though they might have deterred small marauding bands, they would never have stopped a determined assault even by a handful of men. As with most features in the landscape, the real reasons for moated sites are much more complex.

They have a very restricted period of construction, most being built in the late twelfth and thirteenth centuries and in most cases by small local lords or prosperous farmers. They seem to have had a multitude of uses: they provided water for animals, fish were kept in them, they acted as water tanks in the event of fire, they were incorporated into gardens and they also provided some protection against lawless bands at a time when the King's writ was not quite as effective in practice as it was in theory.

But perhaps most of all moats were status symbols. They were a poor alternative to a castle, but nevertheless marked their owners as a class above the mass of the rural peasantry.

The moated Manor Farm at Eltisley, Cambridgeshire, typical of many of the moated sites of Mid Anglia. The house itself dates only from the fifteenth century but the surrounding moat was dug three hundred years before as a status symbol by the owner of an earlier house.

Planning the Food Supply

Certainly by the thirteenth century, though perhaps not in early Saxon times, all the villages in Mid Anglia were surrounded by the characteristic 'open fields', divided into long narrow strips and cultivated in common. Some of these were replaced by sheep pastures in the fifteenth and sixteenth centuries when their parent villages were deserted. More open-field land was transformed in the seventeenth century as new agricultural methods were introduced, but most was enclosed in the eighteenth and nineteenth centuries following formal Acts of Parliament. It might be thought that, as a result, all traces of open-field farming must have gone: yet this is not so at all.

Across hundreds of acres of Mid Anglia the observant traveller can still see the corrugated 'ridge-and-furrow' that marks the former plough

This map of 1600 shows the fields of Gamlingay, Cambridgeshire. On the left are long narrow open strips. In the centre are hedged fields which were formed by the enclosure of former open strips.

ridges of the medieval open-field strips. Today modern agricultural practices have removed and are still slowly removing all signs of these medieval field systems, but there are some clear traces in a few places. The deserted villages such as Canons

Ashby and Clopton, mentioned earlier, have small areas of very fine ridge-and-furrow around them, and a few fields which became pastures still retain the pattern imposed on them by the medieval ploughmen.

More extensive and much

This corrugated field at Wadenhoe, Northamptonshire, shows the arrangement of the medieval strip fields which once existed there.

At Wimpole Hall, Cambridgeshire, the ridge-and-furrow of the medieval open fields of Wimpole still reaches almost to the walls of the house.

more revealing are the extensive spreads of ridge-and-furrow preserved in the parkland around the later great country houses of Mid Anglia. Houses such as Wimpole, near Cambridge (owned by the National Trust), Lamport in Northamptonshire (over which the Trust holds protective covenants), and Althorp, Castle Ashby and Boughton, all in Northamptonshire, and Burghley in Cambridgeshire, have very large areas of ridge-and-furrow within their parks. Close examination has revealed many details of medieval agricultural practices such as access-ways,

headlands (where the plough was turned), as well as special areas left for grazing animals. In just one place, at Soham, Cambridgeshire, medieval fields still remain in cultivation. This is because, as a result of an accident of history, the old fields have survived, though in a modified form. At Soham, the curved strips and access-ways look much as they did seven hundred years ago.

An associated but very different form of medieval cultivation produced 'strip-lynchets'. These appear as rows of terraces, arranged like great stairways across long steep hill slopes. Contrary to popular belief

they are not old vineyards, but arose through medieval strip fields being ploughed along the contours in order to cultivate sloping land which would otherwise have been waste. As steep slopes are relatively rare in Mid Anglia, strip-lynchets are not common. A rare group, on comparatively gentle slopes, is preserved under a glorious beech wood, also a nature reserve, at Wandlebury near Great Shelford in Cambridgeshire; but the best-preserved lie along the chalk escarpment in south Bedfordshire. These include fine sets around the slopes of Castle Hill at Tottenhoe, and

The deserted village of Clopton, Cambridgeshire, where 'pillow mounds' mark the old rabbit warren.

are especially prominent on the valley side to the north of Sharpenhoe Clappers – best seen from the path which links the National Trust car park to the hill top.

There are numerous other aspects of medieval life wonderfully preserved in Mid Anglia. Also at Sharpenhoe Clappers is a large long mound or bank on the southern edge of the beech wood. This was part of a medieval rabbit warren. Above the deserted village of Clopton, Cambridgeshire, there are other examples of these warrens or 'pillow mounds', which provided an 'instant' supply of fresh food for medieval

households. Another even more spectacular rabbit warren is at Higham Ferrers, Northamptonshire, to the north of the parish church in the municipal recreation ground. Local legend has it that this mound, together with its associated ponds, are part of 'Higham Ferrers Castle', and this story is also repeated on modern OS maps. In fact the castle lay a little further to the south, and the mound is actually part of an enclosed rabbit warren owned by the Duchy of Lancaster in medieval times. The ponds which partly enclose the mound tell of yet another aspect of medieval life, for they are the

manorial fish ponds.

Fish was a very important product in Mid Anglia in medieval times. The fens and fenland rivers of course provided vast quantities of fish, not only for the inhabitants of the region, but also for export to places much further afield. In the fourteenth century, for example, fish were regularly sent from the eastern fens to Bedford. However, in western Cambridgeshire, Northamptonshire and Bedfordshire almost every manorial lord and many villages had their own fish ponds as well. These were often highly complex constructions which included

The elaborate dovecote at Willington, Bedfordshire, was built by Sir John Gostwick shortly before 1541 as part of an extensive range including a manor

house and stables. He entertained Henry VIII at Willington in 1541.

breeding ponds or 'stew tanks', dams, sluices and various overflow and supply channels. The finest, not only in Mid Anglia but arguably in England, are those at Harringworth, in northern Northamptonshire, which lie in the valley bottom below the village. The footpath from Harringworth to Arthingworth crosses them and indeed the path actually runs along the top of one of the main dams. These fish ponds were owned by the Knights Templars who held Harringworth in medievel times and the ponds were so large and complex that they were clearly used as commercial fish farms.

Other complex fish ponds exist on either side of the drive to Denney Abbey in Cambridgeshire. These were constructed to provide a constant supply of fish for the inhabitants of the Abbey. Another splendid set of monastic fish ponds survives in the grassland immediately in front of Anglesey Abbey, Cambridgeshire, a National Trust property. The Trust also holds the well-known dovecote at Willington, just east of Bedford. This magnificent stone structure with stepped gables is of sixteenth-century date and was built by Sir John Gostwick, Cardinal Wolsey's Master of the Horse. It contains nesting boxes for 1,500 pigeons and is a comparatively rare survivor of a common structure of medieval times when many lords had such pigeon houses. They provided instant meat and eggs for the noble household and its visitors. Together with the rabbit warrens they were the medieval equivalent of modern deep-freezes. Close to the dovecote are Gostwick's stables, which are almost equally impressive.

Other stone dovecotes accessible to the visitor include one at Wadenhoe in Northamptonshire. Further east, in Cambridgeshire, dovecotes were usually of timber, and square in plan. Few survive now, and of those that do a number were turned into cottages in the eighteenth and nineteenth centuries when the rural

The stables at Willington, Bedfordshire, the only other surviving part of Sir John Gostwick's house. He is buried in the church in the background.

population was expanding rapidly. The most notable is at Manor Farm, Grantchester, just south-east of Cambridge, a building which once belonged to King's College. Most of the wooden dovecotes that survive are of post-medieval date.

Another important feature of the medieval landscape was the windmill. However, windmills are notoriously subject to natural disasters and none of the medieval period remains. The oldest surviving windmill in England still stands at Bourn, Cambridgeshire, and was built in the early seventeenth century. It is a post mill, its machinery as well as its sails rotating on a central post, and as such it represents the older medieval form of windmill, later replaced by the tower mill and the smock mill, where only the sails and cap were turned. Many ruinous tower and smock mills survive, mainly of eighteenth- or nineteenth-century date. The best is at Stevington in Bedfordshire, now fully restored.

The small dovecote at Wadenhoe, Northamptonshire, is perhaps late medieval in date. It still retains the nesting boxes inside.

Windmill, Great Chishill, Cambridgeshire. This post-mill was built in 1819 out of the materials of an older mill on the same site.

Early Castles

Mid Anglia cannot boast of any great medieval castles. A number certainly existed, but time on the whole has treated them badly and little remains to be seen. The great Royal Castle at Northampton was destroyed by the building of the railway in the nineteenth century while that at Bedford only exists as a battered mound. The castle at Wisbech, Cambridgeshire, is now preserved in the name of a circular crescent on the south side of the market place. At Rockingham Castle, the magnificent gatehouse of 1276–91 with its great circular towers survives, as does part of the earlier Norman motte. But all the internal buildings here are of much later date.

On the other hand Mid Anglia does possess a remarkable group of early Norman castles, most of which were erected as huge 'mottes' or conical mounds in the late eleventh or early twelfth centuries and which, for a variety of reasons, were abandoned or altered later. The huge mound on Castle Hill, Cambridge, which looks out over the River Cam to the town below, was built by William the Conqueror after he had taken Cambridge and chose to flaunt his newly won power over the English. A similar mound, built by an early Norman abbot, lies in the parkland on the south side of Ely Cathedral, while another at Huntingdon overlooks the crossing of the River Ouse. Others, built by unknown Norman lords, include the huge motte at Tottenhoe in south Bedfordshire, the motte and massive outworks at Yelden, also in Bedfordshire, and the slightly smaller mound at Lilbourne, in north-west Northamptonshire.

At Castle Camps in south-east Cambridgeshire, an isolated church now stands within the outworks of the remnants of the castle of the medieval Earls of Oxford. The church indicates that this castle attracted a village to its site but both castle and village are abandoned, the village having migrated across its fields to a new position.

Rockingham Castle, Northamptonshire, originally a royal stronghold. Only the great gate house, rebuilt by Edward I in 1276–91, now remains. The castle gradually became a country house and this eighteenth-century view shows various outbuildings alongside the wall. These were removed in a general tidying up in the mid nineteenth century.

Plan of Gateway

The huge earthen mound, surrounding ditch and outer banks are all that remains of a mighty Norman castle at Yelden, Bedfordshire. Its history is quite unknown.

The medieval church of Castle Camps, Cambridgeshire, now stands alone within the earthen ramparts of the great medieval castle of the Earls of Oxford. Both the castle and its associated village were abandoned centuries ago.

By 1730, as this view shows, only a fragment of the ancient Castle Camps remained, built on to a later house. Now both have gone.

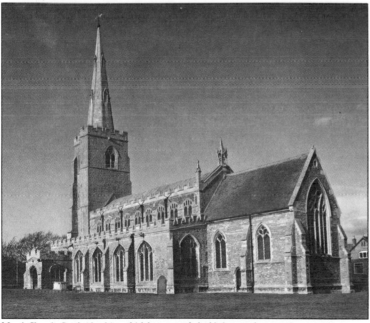

Lowick Church, Northamptonshire. A fine late medieval church built at the expense of three successive members of the Greene family between 1370 and 1470.

Medieval Churches and Monastic Houses

Although the castles of Mid Anglia are now decayed, the mark of the medieval church is still firmly stamped on the landscape. As in other parts of England towers and spires dot the countryside giving us not only a legacy of beautiful buildings, but also a vivid reminder of the all-pervading power and influence of the medieval church. Yet, as with so much else in medieval times, the church was not a static organization. Throughout time its ideas and beliefs were modified, its sources of income changed, and most of all its idea of the proper form for a house of worship was constantly altered.

Few churches are the product of any one period but display a glorious joining of styles and decorations. True, there are some fine late-medieval Perpendicular structures such as those at Burwell and March in Cambridgeshire or Lowick in Northamptonshire, and among earlier almost single-period churches are the thirteenth-century cathedral-like building at Felmersham, Bedfordshire, and the splendid Norman work at Castor, near Peterborough. But perhaps far more interesting and much more typical are those with a multitude of medieval building phases whose shapes help us not only to understand their architectural development but, more fascinatingly, tell of the marvellous inter-relationships between engineers, masons, patrons and worshippers, all working to beautify their world and express their enduring belief in God. Such churches, often the least visited, tell us more about the medieval world and its ideas than do many of the better-known structures.

An example is Orwell, only a mile or two from Wimpole Hall, Cambridgeshire; although it is a very typical parish church, it has a long history which can be unravelled by the casual visitor. The earliest part of

March Church, Cambridgeshire, which has a superb double hammerbeam roof.

The great tower of Burwell Church, Cambridgeshire, is all that remains of a twelfth-century structure. In the fifteenth century it was heightened and the rest of the church completely rebuilt.

Above: Two churches in the same churchyard, at Swaffham Prior, Cambridgeshire. Their existence reflects a combination of lordly piety and rivalry in medieval times.
Below: The chancel at Orwell Church, Cambridgeshire, dominates the rest of this small, otherwise typical parish church. This is because the chancel was erected as a lavish memorial to Sir Simon Burley, lord of the manor and tutor to Richard II, who was executed in 1388.

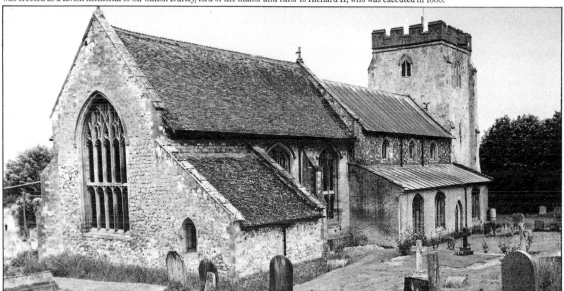

Orwell church is the lower part of its tower, but from the way this joins the rest of the church it is possible to tell how, in the twelfth century, when the first church was erected, it consisted of a squat tower, an aisleless nave and a small chancel. Such a building was more than adequate to house the small numbers of worshippers at Orwell at that period. Then, as the village grew in size and architectural styles and fashions changed, the church was enlarged and rebuilt. In the mid thirteenth century the tower was heightened, and a few years later a north aisle was added. Then, in the early fourteenth century, a south aisle and a porch were built. At the end of the fourteenth century, the old chancel was removed and rebuilt on a larger scale. This was paid for by the then rector, Richard Anlaby, as a memorial to his patron and friend Sir Simon Burley. Burley had been lord of the manor of Orwell and tutor to the young Richard II. He was impeached and executed in 1388 and the new chancel was erected in his memory. As with many churches, little was added to Orwell in the immediate post-Reformation period, or even in the eighteenth century. By the nineteenth century the church was in poor condition and passed through two massive stages of restoration. A very different church is at

Great Brington in Northamptonshire. The main body of the church tells a story similar to that at Orwell and countless others. It was totally rebuilt in the thirteenth century and nothing earlier survives. A number of later features were added, but in the fifteenth century it became the parish church of the Spencer family who had then recently arrived at nearby Althorp from their ancestral home at Wormleighton, Warwickshire. The family fortune had been made by evicting peasants and raising sheep upon the ancestral village lands of the now-deserted parish. Thereafter the church came under the care and use of the Spencers. Sir John Spencer rebuilt the chancel and added chapels to the north and south around 1520. The former became the Spencer family chapel. Within it is one of the most marvellous arrays of aristocratic funeral monuments in England. The effigies of Sir John himself and his wife lie in a chest-tomb, under a canopy, still in medieval style. Four later Spencers are also commemorated by chest-tombs, but the rest are remembered by other, later and sometimes very curious monuments. The memorial to Sir Edward Spencer (died 1656), for instance, portrays a figure rising out of a large urn, while Earl Spencer (d. 1783) is commemorated by a female figure holding a medallion with his profile on it.

As in all parts of Britain, the medieval period in Mid Anglia saw numerous great abbeys flourishing. On the whole, time has treated them badly. Most have now disappeared without trace, or only banks, ditches and scarps mark out their sites. The Cistercian Abbey of Pipewell, in Northamptonshire, is such a place, with only mounds of earth to mark the position of the ancient abbey church. At Sawtry in Cambridgeshire, the site of another Cistercian abbey still retains the traces of the precinct boundary, fish ponds and paddocks, and the same is true of Old Warden in Bedfordshire.

At Delapre, Northampton, nothing but fragments of walling survive, built into the structure of a later house.

Elsewhere, a little more can be seen. The now-redundant church at Canons Ashby is actually part of the nave and north aisle of the former Augustinian priory, founded in about 1150, though almost all the surviving architecture is of about 1230–40. More impressive is St Peter's, Dunstable, Bedfordshire, once the church of another Augustinian priory, founded in 1131. Though again all the eastern half of the original church has now gone, what remains is a memorable structure, basically of the late twelfth century. At Elstow, also in Bedfordshire, part of the church of a house of Benedictine nuns survives, together with a quite remarkable detached bell tower of the fifteenth century. Small fragments of other monastic houses can also be seen. At Anglesey Abbey, now in the care of the National Trust, the dining room is situated within what was probably part of the Augustinian Prior's lodgings, and has two octagonal piers supporting a vaulted stone ceiling.

Elstow Church, Bedfordshire, founded as a nunnery in 1075. The monastic buildings and the east end of the church were demolished in 1580, and the remainder, including much Norman work, was retained as the parish church. An unusual feature is the detached tower or campanile which dates from the fifteenth century.

It is to the Cambridgeshire fenland that the visitor must go to see the best remains of monastic houses in Mid Anglia, and these form a remarkable collection. At the lower end of the scale is Isleham Priory, now in the care of the State. The house was a tiny alien Benedictine priory, founded in the eleventh century and belonging to the French monastery of St Jacut-sur-mer, in Brittany. It was always poor and small, and as a result the typical early Norman chapel was never enlarged, altered or rebuilt. Though now only a shell, it is a marvellous reminder of what must have been a very common form, in the first stages of both monastic and parish churches.

Much less complete, but with a far more complex history is Denney Abbey near Waterbeach in Cambridgeshire, also in the care of the State. The visitor's first impression of the site is of a well-ordered Georgian farmhouse. But this is merely an outer shell wrapped round the remains of a Norman monastic church, now beautifully displayed following a careful restoration. The house was founded in 1160 as a place of retreat for elderly monks from Ely, but shortly afterwards it was acquired by the Knights Templars. In 1294, after the suppression of the Knights Templars, it became a house of Franciscan nuns. In the fourteenth century the nave of the old church was turned into a domestic dwelling, at least part of which was used by the Countess of Pembroke who went to live there with the nuns. It was this domestic use of the former church which enabled it easily to be converted into a farmhouse after the monastery was dissolved in the sixteenth century.

Both Isleham and Denney were minor religious houses. Far more important were the great Benedictine fenland abbeys of Ely, Peterborough, Ramsey and Thorney. At Thorney, as with Dunstable and Elstow, only the nave of the former monastic church survives, and for the same reason: the naves served as parish churches and thus remained intact when other parts of the buildings were destroyed at the Reformation. What remains at Thorney is basically the Norman church, built between 1085 and 1108, but with many later alterations. At Ramsey Abbey much less remains, as the monastic buildings were converted into a house in the early seventeenth century. Part of the thirteenth-century detached Lady Chapel survives, but more important is the fragment of the monastic gatehouse of about 1500, now preserved by the National Trust. This is a highly ornate remnant, clearly intended to announce to visitors the wealth and prestige of the great abbey beyond.

Peterborough Abbey survives almost complete, largely because, unlike most of its fellows, it was raised to cathedral status (in 1541) and so survived the otherwise inevitable orgy of destruction that followed the Dissolution of the Monasteries. The cathedral church is the product of a long process of building following a fire which

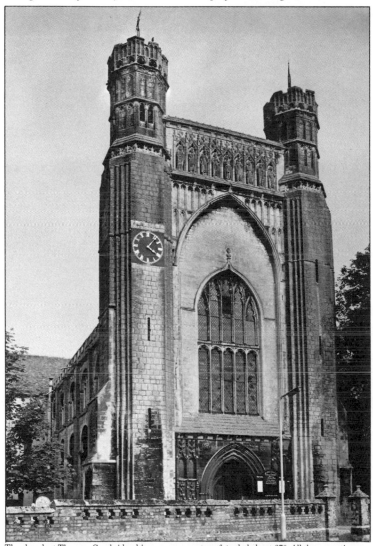

The church at Thorney, Cambridgeshire, was a monastery, founded about 670. All the monastic buildings and the original chancel and central tower were destroyed at the Dissolution; what survives is the part of the original building that was used as a parish church.

destroyed an earlier one in 1116, and it was not completed until 1238. It includes some of the best Norman architecture in Britain. Around the church, fragments of the monastic buildings also survived, the most notable being the great gatehouse which leads to the town centre beyond.

The great glory of Mid Anglia's church buildings is, of course, Ely Cathedral. Like Peterborough and Ramsey it was an ancient Saxon monastery, but it was always far richer than these, partly because its abbots were also always bishops and because they owned and ruled most of the Cambridgeshire fenlands. This secular and religious power, as well as the individuality and piety of the bishops/abbots, is well reflected in the building remains. The present church was started in 1083 and work continued slowly over a hundred years. In its final form, as an entire Norman cathedral of considerable size, it must have been seen as a staggering architectural triumph by the contemporary peasants and the remaining nave and aisles are still overwhelming. However, the church did not remain in this form for long. In 1234 parts of the chancel and aisles were torn down and replaced. This wholesale destruction of large parts of medieval churches, cathedrals and abbeys was, of course, a routine feature of the period. What would today be regarded as vandalism was quite normal in medieval times, and is a reflection of the great differences in attitude to such buildings.

The new work at Ely was completed in 1252 when the church was finally acceptable to its users. Then, on 22 February 1322, disaster struck. The central tower collapsed taking with it part of the chancel. Yet out of its ruins emerged, phoenix-like, what many consider as perhaps the most remarkable piece of religious architecture in Britain: the Octagon. Mere words cannot describe either the details of its structure, nor the emotional impact on any visitor. From

This magnificent gate house is almost all that remains of the great fenland abbey of Ramsey, Cambridgeshire. Its lavish decoration shows the great wealth of the abbey shortly before it was dissolved by Henry VIII.

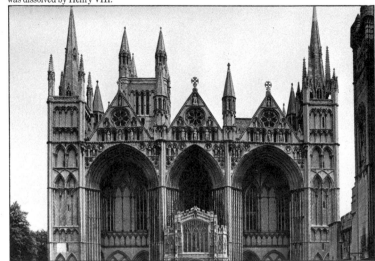

Peterborough Cathedral, one of the great medieval fenland abbeys, saved from destruction at the Dissolution by being raised in 1541 to the rank of cathedral.

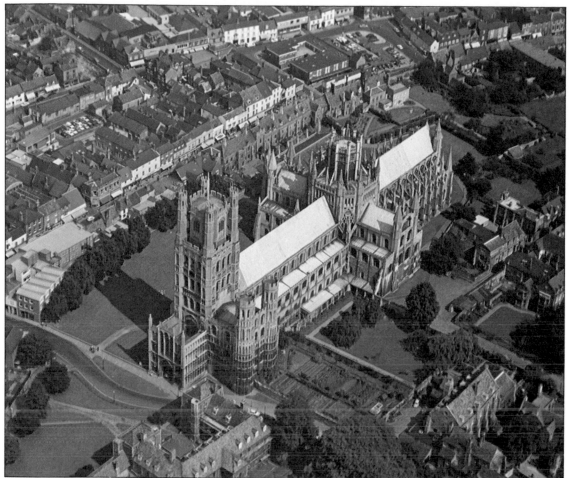

Ely from the air. The Cathedral dominates the adjacent town which would not have existed without it.

Exterior and interior views of the Octagon, Ely Cathedral, perhaps the greatest piece of fourteenth-century architecture in Britain.

the Norman nave, the crossing explodes into towering space with pillars raking skywards between broad tall windows before breaking out into a fan-like set of ribs which support the smaller brightly lit 'lantern'. There is nothing in Mid Anglia that can stir the heart more than the Octagon at Ely. The later work there, including even the magnificent Lady Chapel of 1335–53, is pallid in comparison.

One lesser-known though interesting aspect of the ecclesiastical buildings of Mid Anglia are the late medieval collegiate churches. The monastic houses were very largely founded and supported by the gifts of money and land from the upper classes. But by the fourteenth century attitudes to the church were changing. Monastic houses lost favour and new ideas of piety appeared. Thus endowments which would earlier have been given to monasteries in return for prestige, status, or merely insurance for the hereafter, were presented to parish churches. The money was used in various ways depending upon the size of the gift and the importance of the benefactor. A little money would pay for a single priest to pray for the souls of the benefactor and his family. More might provide a priest or even a group of clerics as well as a specially built 'chantry chapel'. Such chapels are of course very common and among the most notable are two at St Mary's,

Higham Ferrers College in the eighteenth century. It was already then ruinous, having been dissolved at the Reformation.

The Bede House, Higham Ferrers, Northamptonshire. It was founded in 1431 together with a school and a college of secular canons by Thomas Chichele, Archbishop of Canterbury, to honour and endow his birthplace.

Luton. However, at the highest level of benefaction a college of clerics (often attached to an existing church) could be provided in honour of the donor.

In Northamptonshire a whole group of such colleges was founded in the late fourteenth and fifteenth centuries. The most magnificent was at Fotheringhay, where the new church of cathedral-like proportions was provided by Edmund Langley, son of Edward III, and by Langley's son, Edward of York. As with the monastic houses, these colleges were dissolved at the Reformation and now only the nave (actually the original parish church) remains at Fotheringhay. The chancel and all the attached collegiate buildings were pulled down in the sixteenth century. Yet what remains is a marvellous piece of Perpendicular architecture, as good as any in the rest of England. Fotheringhay was a royal college and thus, inevitably, most magnificent. Another college was founded in 1431 at Higham Ferrers by Thomas Chichele, Archbishop of Canterbury, who was born at Higham. Chichele also founded a school and a 'bedehouse' or old men's hospital there. Both still survive, but the college is now in ruins, though protected and open to the public. The gatehouse, part of the chapel and the foundations of the hall are visible. A third college was founded at Cotterstock by John Giffard, a Canon of York, in 1377. Here too, all the

Detail with mourning figures.

collegiate buildings have gone, but the rebuilt chancel of the older parish church remains. It is huge, dominating the rest of the building, while inside it is lofty and wonderfully illuminated by great windows with highly decorated tracery.

There is one final group of quasi-religious monuments of a very special kind in Mid Anglia, the Eleanor Crosses; one is at Geddington, and the other is on the road south from Northampton at Delapre Abbey in Northamptonshire. They were erected by Edward I in memory of his wife Eleanor, who died at Harby, Lincolnshire, in November 1290. Her body was taken to London for burial and the king set up lavishly decorated crosses at the places where the funeral cortège halted overnight. Only three crosses now survive, two of them in Northamptonshire, and that at Geddington is the best preserved.

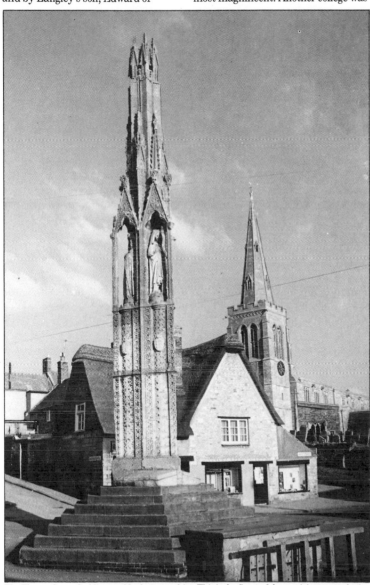

The Eleanor Cross, Geddington, Northamptonshire. This is the finest of the surviving crosses built to mark the journey in 1290 of the body of Queen Eleanor home to Westminster from Harby, in Lincolnshire, where she died. The intricate but restrained decoration of the lower part is notable.

Manor Houses

Almost nothing is recognizable of the medieval lay people of Mid Anglia. There are, it is true, a number of small fourteenth- and fifteenth-century manor houses, while some of the greater country houses have fragments of late medieval work in them. But in both instances the old structures are covered by later alterations and little can be appreciated without detailed study. The small hovel-like structures of medieval peasants survive merely as low earthworks in some deserted villages, especially those where limestone was freely available for their foundations. Such foundations exist at the former villages of Kirby and Snorscombe, in Northamptonshire. Elsewhere, only the expert can be sure that, for example, the house on Barrington Green in Cambridgeshire actually retains within its structure evidence that shows it was a wealthy medieval farmer's 'aisled hall' of the fourteenth century.

Within country houses such as Boughton and Deene, in Northamptonshire, the later changes are wrapped around medieval cores, and one can still see the much-altered great halls which were the social centres for life in all the lordly residences of the period. In one or two places more complete structures remain. At Northborough near Peterborough are the remains of the mid fourteenth-century manor house which contains not only a magnificent hall, but also a splendid gatehouse dominating the approach, a feature which was common in later medieval times. Also near Peterborough is Longthorpe Tower, now in the care of the State. This is a somewhat extraordinary find in this part of England and is more reminiscent of the far North. The site was that of a manor house of which the late thirteenth-century hall survives. Then, about 1300, a tall three-storey tower was added, making it look rather like the defensive tower houses

of the Scottish borders. Here, however, defence may not have been the major consideration. The prestige attaching to such a tower – whose builder was after all the steward of Peterborough Abbey – may have been paramount. A similar tower is embedded in the surrounding house at Southwick Hall in Northamptonshire, and this too seems more a status symbol than a defensive measure.

The status-endowing qualities of mock fortifications survived into later medieval times, and indeed beyond. Our best example is at Buckden, in Cambridgeshire, the site of one of the great palaces of the Bishops of Lincoln. The whole palace was rebuilt in the late fifteenth century, though now only the gatehouse and the Great Tower survive, all in red brick. The tower is remarkable, and with its angled turrets and crenellated parapets looks at first sight like a major defensive keep. Then one sees the broad mullioned windows and huge stepped chimney stacks and realizes that it has no defensive capacity at all and is merely a great medieval dignitary's symbol of power.

Growth of the Towns

Of all the facets of the landscape of Mid Anglia in medieval times, probably the most important and certainly the most obvious were the towns. As noted earlier, the first towns were all planned either by the Danes or the late Saxon kings or by various lords soon after the Norman Conquest. This was only the beginning, and in the twelfth and thirteenth centuries a host of new towns appeared, most being deliberately planned by the great lords who owned the lands on which they stood. Ely and Wisbech in Cambridgeshire were both planned anew as towns in the early twelfth century, both by Bishops of Ely. Peterborough appeared in the early twelfth century, arising outside the great abbey. Indeed its very name

shows that it was intended to be the borough of the Church of St Peter, whereas the earlier village there was known as Medhampstead.

In Northamptonshire, Daventry (of the mid twelfth century) and Brackley (by 1173) are both 'new', while Oundle is almost certainly another medieval foundation. St Neots (1113–22) and St Ives (1110), in Cambridgeshire, are similarly new foundations, as is Dunstable in Bedfordshire. At all these places little or nothing seems to survive of the medieval period, apart from the parish churches. Yet their planned origins are still clearly marked in the existing street layout.

The rectangular market places at St Neots and Ely both still remain; at St Neots it is much as it was formed in the twelfth century. The market place at Ely is now only a

fraction of its former size, having been largely built over by merchants who turned their market stalls into permanent shops. Yet the narrow lanes that exist on the western side of the market place are actually the original walk-ways between the medieval stalls. Peterborough still retains its great planned market square, as do Brackley and Daventry. The market place at St Ives has also been greatly reduced by later encroachment, but the town retains its magnificent bridge across the River Ouse, built in the fourteenth century to link it to its hinterland and so increase its prosperity. Of the older Saxon towns in Mid Anglia there is similarly little to see of the medieval period with one remarkable exception: Cambridge. Here the university and college buildings are of such beauty and interest as to overshadow all

other towns in the region – and indeed those of regions far beyond.

Histories and guidebooks are available in great profusion and collectively they seem to contain all that can be said about Cambridge. Even so, the visitor is likely to be overwhelmed by first impressions of the city and certainly cannot take in all it offers without staying there for weeks rather than days. For the casual traveller the eye is inevitably and justly drawn to the glories of King's College Chapel (1446–1515), the magnificent splendour of Trinity Great Court, the outrageous Gothic of the Bridge of Sighs (1831) and St John's Cripps Building (1963–67). Yet there are other, quieter and more intimate places such as Jesus College, constructed out of the remains of an older structure belonging to the Franciscan friars.

Top: St Ives Bridge, Cambridgeshire, built in the fourteenth century to link the planned town of St Ives with its hinterland across the River Ouse to the south. The small building in the centre of the bridge was a chapel.
Above: King's College Chapel, Cambridge, perhaps the finest, and certainly the best-known, of all the buildings in Cambridge.

For beyond the sheer beauty of the architecture, the Cambridge colleges share one overriding feature. They were designed for communal education at a time when the only models for such communal living were the great medieval monastic houses. Thus, even the modern colleges imitate a medieval monastic way of life. Their enclosed courts are the equivalent of the cloisters. Their protected gates, gatehouses and high walls cut off the occupants from the dangers and temptations of the outside world. Their great dining halls preserve the traditional medieval way of eating, while their ranges of rooms follow the concept of monastic cells. Even their chapels remind us that they were created in an age when the church had a monopoly of education and theology was the basis of almost all teaching.

One other important, but often forgotten, feature of Cambridge needs to be stressed. As was noted earlier, the town was founded by the Danes as a commercial centre in the ninth century. The university did not arrive in Cambridge until the thirteenth century. Thus for four hundred years Cambridge had an existence which did not involve the university. During that time, because of its local position and its navigable river, it became a national and even an international market centre. In late Saxon times Cambridge exploded from its original core, close to Magdalene Bridge, and spread southwards along the eastern side of the River Cam. By the twelfth century, the area now occupied by the great beauties of King's, Queens', Clare, St John's and Trinity Colleges was divided into narrow streets and lanes, lined with merchants' houses and warehouses, and leading down to busy wharves along the river.

From the thirteenth century onwards a process unique in English towns occurred. The university and the colleges acquired by sale or grant prime sites in what was then the commercial heart of a great inland port and marketing centre. As the colleges grew richer, they expanded and gradually took over this commercial centre whose functions were pushed eastwards, to the present shopping centre and market place. By the sixteenth century the colleges had acquired almost all the riverside land and had created the magnificent structures which still exist.

The older market town of Cambridge was completely disrupted by the arrival of the university. And yet, even today, faint traces of its earlier history still remain. Some of the lanes that ran down to the medieval wharves and parts of some of the linking streets have managed to survive, squeezed in between the college buildings. Garrett Hostel Lane, Queen's Lane and Trinity Lane are all remnants of a much older town.

Bridge of Sighs and New Court, St John's College, Cambridge. Although the bridge is world-famous, New Court is less well known but dates from the same year – 1831.

Queen's Lane, Cambridge, in the early nineteenth century. Then, as now, it was a cul-de-sac running between St Catharine's and Queens' Colleges, but in earlier medieval times it was one of the main thoroughfares of the great inland port of Cambridge.

Right: Cambridge in 1574. It is still a medieval town, but already the colleges are established on the former prime commercial area along the River Cam, and the rest of the town is jammed uncomfortably in the eastern half.

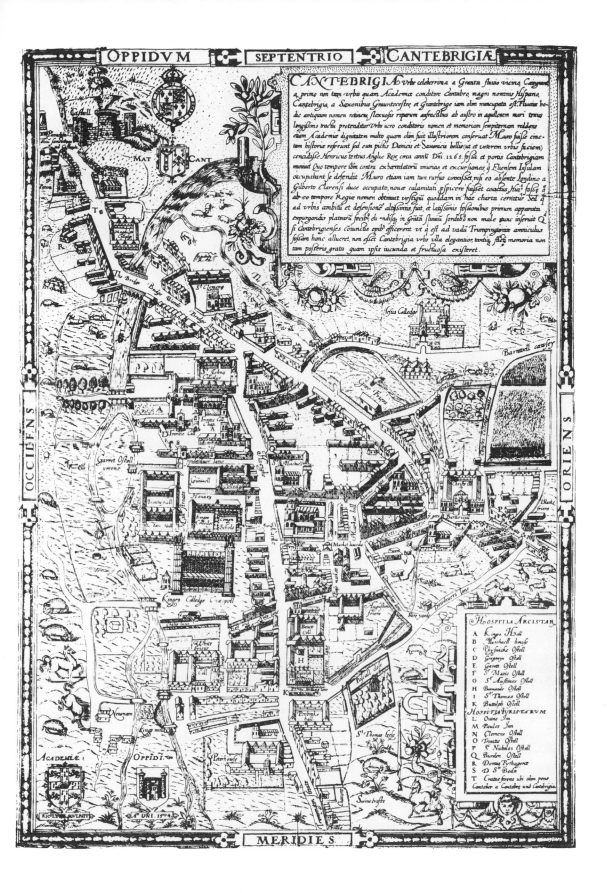

THE MODERN LANDSCAPE

By the mid sixteenth century a combination of underlying geology and early history had imposed on the rural landscape of Mid Anglia a variety of contrasting aspects. In the north-west, the fenlands remained much as they had for centuries, a largely undrained and marshy wilderness. They provided summer grazing for cattle and sheep, endless supplies of peat, fish, wildfowl and sedge, and their meandering rivers made up for the almost total lack of adequate roads in the area. These resources were exploited by the inhabitants of the compact villages which lay all around the fen edges and on the clay islands within them.

Over most of the rest of the region, the villages were mainly surrounded by their open fields, except where the desertion of villages had led to their replacement by large sheep pastures or where, in land cleared from former woodland, small enclosed fields dominated. Within this landscape of villages and fields, there were no great country houses and no parkland. All the towns were relatively small, little more than large villages by modern standards. It was a landscape that, by and large, would be unfamiliar to a traveller of today. Yet within three hundred years the whole of the region was to be transformed beyond all recognition by the impact of new ideas, techniques and ways of life which swept over Mid Anglia. Some of these changes were on a relatively small scale; some were immense.

Draining the Fens

One of the most profound changes was the drainage and reclamation of the fenlands. Although there had been small-scale reclamation along the fen edge in medieval times, neither the technology nor the co-operative spirit was available to carry out the large-

scale and co-ordinated work necessary to achieve proper reclamation. By the early seventeenth century both requirements existed and work began –albeit very slowly and with numerous unforeseen difficulties. The result was the formation of the present fenland landscape.

The first major work was carried out in the 1630s by a group of Adventurers, under the patronage of the Fourth Earl of Bedford, who put up, or 'adventured' capital for drainage work in return for allotments of newly reclaimed land. The initial efforts were directed to the construction of new and large-scale water channels which would both carry the water of upland rivers across the fens without flooding them, and remove water from the fens themselves. The greatest of these works were the Old Bedford River (completed 1637) and the New Bedford River (completed 1651) which run roughly parallel to each other for 22 miles across the fens from Earith in Cambridgeshire to Denver in Norfolk. These two gigantic channels not only shortened the course of the River Ouse and carried its normal flow safely to the sea, but in

the land between them – 'The Washes' – provided a vast reservoir where surplus floodwater was, and still is, stored, thus preventing it from emptying into the adjacent fenlands. Amongst the large internal drains also constructed in the mid seventeenth century which still survive are the Twenty Foot Drain and the Forty Foot or Vermuyden's Drain, both near Chatteris, Cambridgeshire. (Vermuyden was the Dutch engineer who was in charge of all this work, having previously worked in the Isle of Axholme in Lincolnshire.)

Once these drains and channels were completed by the 1650s, the fens were adjudged to be 'drained'. The Adventurers were given their allotments (hence the place name Adventurers' Fen), and reclamation began. Thousands of acres of land were divided into rectangular fields and edged by drains, new farmsteads were established within them, and a new landscape began to emerge.

But by the end of the seventeenth century disaster threatened the area, largely because of a phenomenon which had not been foreseen: peat shrinkage. As the land was reclaimed and water removed, the

Caroli II. Regis.

Chap. 17.

An Act for setling the Dreining of the Great Level of the Fenns, called *Bedford Level.*

Hereas certaine Moores, Marshes, Fenny and Low surrounded Grounds within the Counties of Northampton, Norfolk, Suffolk, Lincoln, Cambridge & Huntington, and the Isle of Ely, were called the Great Level of the Fenns; And after several fruitless Undertakings for Dreining the same, were upon the Desires of many persons of Worth and Interessed in the same, declared to be a Great and Noble Work, and of much Concernment to the whole Countrey, and at their earnest desire undertaken to be Dreined by Francis late Earl of Bedford, according to a Law of Sewers made at Kings Lynne in the Sixth year of the Reign of the late King Charles of glorious memory; which said Level is bounded as followeth,

Hmm 2   (viz)

Far left: William, Fifth Earl and First Duke of Bedford (1613–1700), the greatest landowner in the fens in the mid seventeenth century and titular head of the Adventurers. His father, the Fourth Earl, began the first co-ordinated drainage of the fens, and he saw its completion. Their name is commemorated in the Bedford Levels and the Bedford Rivers.

Above left: Title page of the General Drainage Act, 1663. This Act established the complex administrative machinery necessary to continue the drainage of the fens after the great construction work of the previous 25 years.

Above: Sir Cornelius Vermuyden, engineer and genius (1595–1683), the man who conceived, designed and carried out the seventeenth-century drainage of the eastern fenlands.

peat covering the fens dried, shrank, compacted and then blew away in the strong fenland gales. The land surface fell dramatically, often as much as six feet in as many years. On the other hand, the main drains and rivers had to be kept at their original height to allow for normal flow. These unforeseen circumstances produced what is now a typical fenland feature, the high-level drain. This, carefully embanked, flows well above the surrounding land; it is best seen on the Bedford Rivers near Mepal and Manea in Cambridgeshire, where the rivers are now more than twenty feet above the fens.

The peat shrinkage produced enormous difficulties. Not only did the drains and rivers have to be protected by banks to prevent them flooding the lower land, but, more important, water on this land could no longer flow into the drains

The Cambridgeshire Fens: a typical view of the rich farmland and straight drainage ditches. The light-coloured band in the background is the bed of a former river.

Drainage mill, Conington, Cambridgeshire, 1853. This is an example of the large mills which dotted the fenlands in the eighteenth and nineteenth centuries. The large circular feature on the right contained the scoop wheel which lifted the water.

and rivers. By 1700, peat shrinkage was taking place on such a scale as to threaten the whole future of the fens. They were saved by the introduction of windmills or, rather, wind-driven lifting machines. During the mid eighteenth century hundreds of tall windmills, driving large-diameter wheels with slats on their circumferences, were erected all over the fens. The slatted wheels scooped water from the fields and lower drains into the higher drains and rivers. Today only one of these mills survives. It is at Wicken Fen Nature Reserve

and is maintained by the National Trust. But it is not typical for it is a very small example; most were very much larger, and this wind pump actually dates only from 1907. The introduction of these lifting machines saved the fens and indeed led to further reclamation. By the early nineteenth century all but a few small areas had been drained and put to agriculture, and countless more farmsteads had appeared, scattered across the fenland.

Yet still all was not well. As drainage became more efficient and

more land was reclaimed, the peat shrank even more. By the end of the eighteenth century the wind-driven machines could not cope, for not only was the height that they could lift water limited, the demands made on them by landowners proved too much. Attempts were made to improve matters by erecting groups of two or three lifting machines working together, but these were not successful. Disaster was again close, yet was averted once more by the introduction of new technology: this time it was the steam engine. The first

Scoop wheel under construction at Benwick, Cambridgeshire, in 1900. Though apparently inefficient, such wheels, driven first by wind power and then by steam engines, were the only method of draining the fens for over two hundred years.

steam engine, still driving a scoop wheel, was erected at Swaffham Prior in Cambridgeshire in 1821. Within a few years, dozens more were built all the way across the fens. After 1850 the old scoop wheels were replaced by centrifugal pumps, which were much more efficient.

These great engines, housed in huge brick structures, became a familiar sight in the fens in the nineteenth century. Now all but one have been abandoned and many completely destroyed. The survivor, at Stretham, Cambridgeshire, was built

in 1831; it is now preserved and open to the public. The mighty engine, with its massive cylinder, spin wheel, rocker beam, boilers and scoop wheel, is housed in a towering brick structure. Nowhere on the fens can one better appreciate the power of nineteenth-century technology in conquering the watery wastes. Elsewhere, only the abandoned engine houses remain; a notable survivor stands on the Downham–Welney road, close to the New Bedford River, to the north-west of Ely. On the walls of the latter building

is an inscription of 1830 which encapsulates the influence of steam on drainage:

'These Fens have oft times been by
water draun'd
Science a remedy in Water found
The powers of Steam She said shall be
employ'd
And the Destroyer by Itself destroy'd.'

From the beginning of the present century these steam engines were gradually replaced by less prepossessing, but much more

Above: Cutting reeds. Another valuable product of the fens, the reeds were harvested on a large scale and used for thatching almost every building in the area until the arrival in the nineteenth century of cheap slates.

efficient diesel engines. These in turn are being replaced by electric pumps. The small sheds housing the machinery for these more modern methods of removing water are hardly noticed by most fenland visitors, but without them, the rich farmlands of the eastern fens would revert to waste in a few short months.

A particularly neat example of the developing technology

A nineteenth-century drawing of peat being stacked. After cutting it was stacked and allowed to dry before being transported, often by barge, to the homes of the workers.

of fen drainage is to be seen at Prickwillow, near Ely. There, the first engine house, built in the 1830s, stands next to a much larger engine house erected in the 1880s to take a bigger and much more efficient steam engine. Now the latter building is home to a powerful diesel engine. Yet even this is now disused. Its modern replacement, an electric pump, is housed in a small modern brick

Above: Diesel engine and pump, Prickwillow, Cambridgeshire. This machinery was installed in the 1930s in the building erected in the 1880s for steam engines. It was in turn superseded in the 1960s by an electric pump. The building is now a museum.
Above left: A peat digger, about 1900. Peat was one of the major natural resources of the fenlands.

building behind it.

Alongside the pumps for removing water many new drains had to be constructed and rivers re-aligned. The present course of the River Nene, from Peterborough to Guyhirn, was cut in 1728. The straight section of the River Ouse between Ely and Littleport dates from 1827, while the North Level Main Drain in the north of Cambridgeshire was dug in 1834.

Drainage channels have always needed to be cleaned out and re-cut. Originally the work was done by hand, and today it is carried out by drag-line. In this photograph, taken about 1897, Victorian technology is seen at work in the shape of a steam-driven bucket-dredger.

The New Agriculture

Outside the fenlands the landscape of Mid Anglia was also massively reorganized in the three centuries after 1550. The major feature was the total removal of the medieval or strip fields and their replacement by the familiar hedged fields of the present landscape. The process of enclosure had, of course, been started by the sheep farmers of the fourteenth and fifteenth centuries. It continued, albeit on a limited scale, during the seventeenth century and the first half of the eighteenth.

Around 1750, the process speeded up, and in little under a century the modern countryside took shape. It is difficult, even now, to imagine the impact of this process, not only on the landscape but on the people involved. In many places an environment and a whole way of life,

established for perhaps almost a thousand years, were swept away in the space of a year or so. And it was all done with scant regard for the wishes of any but the major landowners – and caused considerable social disruption and personal hardship and tragedy. Yet without it the basis of modern agriculture could never have been established and our countryside might have looked far less attractive than it does. If the enclosure of the ancient field systems had had to wait until the twentieth century, the now well-established democratic process of consultation and discussion would not only have lengthened the final achievement, but would have probably produced a very different countryside! As it was, a new landscape of hedged fields, straight roads and brick and stone farmsteads was laid out with a minimum of effective objections in the course of a

few short years.

Nor was this new landscape confined to the areas of the old open strip fields. The influence of the enclosures spread much wider. Any open land was likely to be ruthlessly redesigned. In north Cambridgeshire, for example, the great heathlands in the Soke of Peterborough were cut up into fields – to the despair of the tragic poet John Clare who lived in the area – while the downlands of south Cambridgeshire were divided and ploughed up, leaving only Newmarket Heath. Because of its racing tradition and the power of the Jockey Club it survived as an oasis of grassland in a sea of arable. In Northamptonshire, too, what remained of the great medieval forests of Rockingham, Salcey and Whittlewood were cut down, leaving relatively few patches of woodland to remind us of the past.

Villages of Mid Anglia

The villages also took on their present appearance between 1550 and 1850. Although most villages can boast at least one medieval house, often hidden away under later alterations, the great majority of the domestic buildings in the region's villages are of seventeenth-century and later date. The neat white-plastered and thatched cottages of south Cambridgeshire, the stone-built houses of Northamptonshire and the harsh brick farmsteads of the fenland villages almost all date from after 1600. The earliest of these are mainly of the seventeenth century and, despite their cottage appearance, were usually built by relatively wealthy farmers; little survives of the dwellings of the lower orders of society. Later on many of these farm houses were subdivided into cottages for labourers when the farmers themselves moved into new and more up-to-date houses, either situated in the newly enclosed fields or in the villages. These early houses tend to be long and narrow, only one room deep,

The tragic poet John Clare (1793–1864), born at Helpston, near Peterborough. In his verse he expressed his despair and anguish over the destruction of his native heaths as they were divided into new fields and put under the plough in the early nineteenth century.

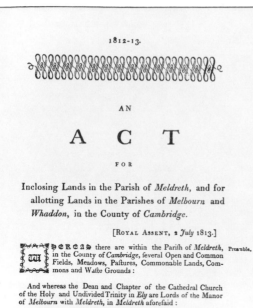

1812-13.

AN

A C T

FOR

Inclosing Lands in the Parish of *Meldreth*, and for
allotting Lands in the Parishes of *Melbourn* and
Whaddon, in the County of *Cambridge*.

[ROYAL ASSENT, 2 July 1813.]

WHEREAS there are within the Parish of *Meldreth*, Preamble.
in the County of *Cambridge*, several Open and Common
Fields, Meadows, Pastures, Commonable Lands, Com-
mons and Waste Grounds :

And whereas the Dean and Chapter of the Cathedral Church
of the Holy and Undivided Trinity in *Ely* are Lords of the Manor
of *Melbourn* with *Meldreth*, in *Meldreth* aforesaid :

And whereas *Wortham Hitch*, Esquire, is Lord of the Manor
of *Melbourn* with *Melreth*, *Argentines* and *Trayles*, in *Meldreth*
aforesaid :

And whereas *Joshua Fitch*, Esquire, is Lord of the Manor of
Sheene, in *Meldreth* aforesaid :

And whereas *Christopher Pemberton*, Esquire, is Lord of the
Manor of *Veyseys* otherwise *Veyseyes*, in *Meldreth* aforesaid :

111.   A   And

The title pages of the Acts of Enclosure for
Meldreth and Orwell, Cambridgeshire, 1813 and
1836. Hundreds of such Acts empowered the
alteration of the Mid Anglian landscape on a
scale never seen before or since.

6 WILL. IV.——SESS. 1836.

AN

A C T

For inclosing Lands in the Parish of *Orwell* in the
County of *Cambridge*, and for commuting the Tithes
of the said Parish.

[ROYAL ASSENT, MARCH 30TH, 1836.]

WHEREAS there are within the parish of *Orwell* in the county Preamble.
of *Cambridge* divers open fields and commonable and waste
lands and grounds, and divers inclosed lands and homesteads :

And whereas *John Bendyshe* Esquire is or claims to be lord of the
manor of *Orwell* aforesaid :

And whereas the said *John Bendyshe* as such lord of the said manor
of *Orwell* is entitled to the soil of the waste lands within such manor :

And whereas the master fellows and scholars of the college of the
Holy and Undivided Trinity within the town and university of Cambridge, of King Henry the Eighth's foundation, are patrons of the
rectory and parish church of *Orwell* aforesaid :
No. 3.

A

And

and betray no pretence at achieving
an ordered or regular design. The later
farmhouses, which by the eighteenth
century were built of brick or stone,
are not only larger but are two rooms
deep, and they have symmetrical
front elevations with central
doorways and balancing windows, a
style which marked out their owners
as wealthy and fashionable people.

The layouts of the villages
themselves also changed markedly
at this time. This was the result of
almost continuous population
increase, especially from the mid
eighteenth century onwards. Villages
tended to become much bigger than
before, and also to be more tightly
packed with dwellings. A fine example
of this is Meldreth in south
Cambridgeshire. Until as late as the
early nineteenth century, Meldreth
kept its medieval form, consisting of
no less than seven separate nuclei,
scattered along a two-mile winding
road. In less than eighty years,
expansion of the village resulting from

a doubling of its population turned it
into a continuous 'linear' settlement.

Many villages also lost their
ancient greens during this period
when they were enclosed and built
over. Orwell, also in Cambridgeshire,
has no green today, but the street
name Town Green Lane suggests that
it once did. This was indeed so, until
1836 when it was completely covered
by cottages and gardens.

The Church of Strixton, Northamptonshire. Once the centre of a flourishing village, it now stands almost alone in the fields. The sheep in the foreground are grazing on the remains of an elaborate sixteenth-century garden belonging to the adjacent manor house. The house and gardens were abandoned in the seventeenth century.

Despite the overall growth in population, villages also shrank in size during these centuries. Strixton in Northamptonshire now only consists of the parish church and a small handful of houses. Yet a map of 1588 shows that it was then a large and flourishing village. It shrank almost to nothing in the mid seventeenth century when the major landowner enclosed its medieval fields and deprived most of its inhabitants of their livelihood.

A few villages disappeared completely, some quite recently, though the reasons for this are unclear. Luddington-in-the-Brook, in east Northamptonshire, consists of

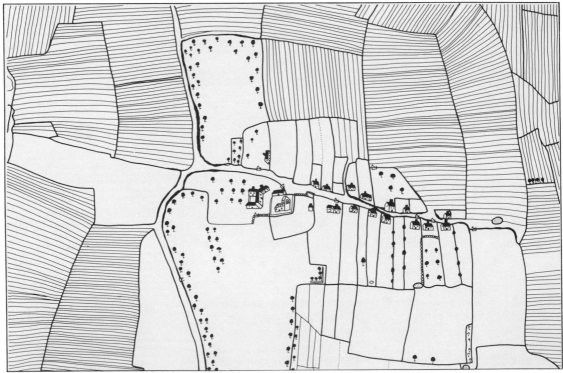

Drawing based on a map of Strixton, Northamptonshire, 1588. At that time the village, though small, still existed, surrounded by its ancient open fields. Within a few years the fields had been enclosed and the village dwindled away almost to nothing.

nothing but the medieval church, the adjacent Church Farm and a row of nineteenth-century cottages. But as late as 1830 there were still half a dozen other farms and a group of cottages, all of which have since disappeared, the last farm being pulled down in 1950. No-one appears to know why this happened, nor has anyone mentioned that it was taking place. There are many puzzles in the history of the landscape which we still cannot explain.

Mid Anglia has a number of very special villages whose appearance and layout are the result of the work of great and powerful lords. For a variety of reasons, but usually to improve the amenities of their estates, these people often changed existing villages out of all recognition. At Madingley in Cambridgeshire the village is made up of two quite separate parts. In one place are the church, two farms and a few cottages, while some distance away is the rest of the village with its public house. Until the mid

eighteenth century the village was of quite a different shape and consisted of a single long street. Then, in 1756, the Cotton family, who owned the adjacent Madingley Hall, commissioned Capability Brown to lay out a park. Brown cut a swathe through the centre of the village, replaced the houses with a serpentine lake and clumps of trees, and thus provided a long wood-edged 'view' from the house.

In Northamptonshire in the early nineteenth century, the owners of Easton Neston House, near Towcester, decided to improve the tiny village of Hulcote which lay nearby. They removed all the existing houses set around an irregular green, changed the green itself into a triangular piece of land, and built the most delightful set of 'Gothicky' cottages along two sides of it. An even more remarkable change occurred at Ashton, near Oundle, in Northamptonshire. Until the late nineteenth century the village lay along a short street with small greens

at either end. Then, around 1900, the Rothschild family, owners of the nearby Ashton Wold House, determined to improve the living conditions of their tenants. They removed the old village completely and laid out a new one round a central green edged by chestnut trees. The new houses and the public house were all built of high-quality stone, with neatly thatched roofs. The result was a typical 'olde-worlde' village of a type that never previously existed.

Even more unreal, yet very typical of Victorian attitudes to both the past and to contemporary society, is Old Warden in Bedfordshire, which was totally rebuilt in the mid nineteenth century by Lord Ongley. Here, brick and tile houses are mixed with timber-framed and thatched cottages in a delightful unworldly way. Perhaps less overwhelming are the neatly thatched estate cottages in nearby Southill, erected by the Whitbread family in the late eighteenth and early nineteenth centuries.

Madingley Church, Cambridgeshire, now at one end of a village split in two parts by a wedge of parkland, ordered in 1756 by the landowner and designed by Capability Brown.

Estate cottages at Southill, Bedfordshire, built in the late seventeenth century by the Whitbread family. Purely artificial 'villages' such as this one, created by great landowners, present an image of the 'Olde Worlde' village that rarely existed in fact.

The best instance of a completely new village is at Wimpole in Cambridgeshire. There the hall and church stand alone in the extensive parkland. Yet the very existence of the church (which, despite its superficial appearance, contains medieval work) implies that there was once a village around it. And indeed there was a village until the seventeenth century. At that time Wimpole village consisted of a number of different parts or nuclei – one around the church, another to the south-west, a third to the south, a fourth to the north of the hall and another well to the north-east. The part around the church was removed in the mid seventeenth century, when the hall was rebuilt by Sir Thomas Chicheley, and was replaced by a formal garden. The two parts to the south and south-west were cleared away in the 1730s when Charles Bridgeman laid out the park there, and the section of the village north of the hall disappeared in the 1750s when Capability Brown extended the park. The last section was finally removed in the early nineteenth century during another

New Wimpole, Cambridgeshire, a new 'village' built in the 1840s as a replacement for the medieval one which had been destroyed piecemeal over the previous two hundred years during the process of emparking.

phase of landscaping. Finally, in the 1840s, a replacement village, New Wimpole, was laid out on the main Cambridge – Biggleswade road to the south of the park. The semi-detached Tudoresque estate cottages of this village still exist.

The result of all this work was to make Wimpole one of the finest pieces of parkland in Britain. But because of the long process of development, the park is much more than this. For preserved in the grassland around the hall are the remains of three parts of the former village with the streets, house-sites and gardens visible as low banks and ditches. In addition, the old roads, now slight hollow-ways, still survive, as do considerable areas of medieval plough ridges from the former strip fields. Numerous other features include the remains of the seventeenth-century formal gardens north of the hall, and the mound which supported the medieval parish windmill. The National Trust holds, in Wimpole Park, an extraordinary piece of fossilized landscape.

Sir John Soane (1753–1837). He was employed in the 1790s by Philip York, Third Earl of Hardwicke, to remodel Wimpole Hall, Cambridgeshire. The interior of the house today owes much to him, particularly the wonderful Yellow Drawing Room.

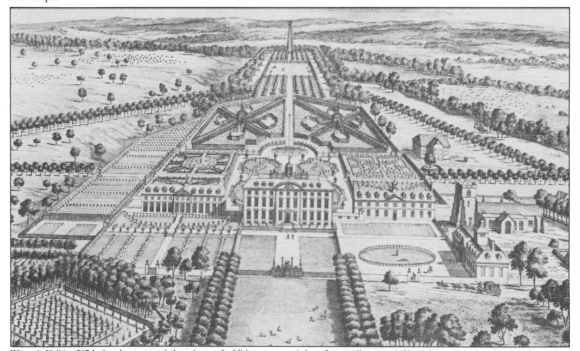

Wimpole Hall in 1707, before the structural alterations and additions were carried out. It was still surrounded by elaborate formal gardens which were swept away in 1752.

Great Houses and Their Parks

Other great houses in the region are also surrounded by parks with remains which, though not particularly obvious to the casual visitor, give fascinating insights into the past history of the area. At Boughton, in Northamptonshire, not only is there the site of the old village of Boughton – now reduced to slight banks and scarps – but, much more important, the park containing the remains of a great garden laid out in the French style by Ralph, First Duke of Montagu in the late seventeenth and early eighteenth centuries, and then abandoned and turned into parkland in the mid 1740s. The remains consist of high-level 'canals', terraces, sunken basins and even a great 'mount'. A still earlier garden, which includes flights of terraces, ponds and mounts, exists in the parkland at Holdenby in Northamptonshire. This was laid out in the 1580s by Sir Christopher Hatton, who was Lord Chancellor

from 1587 to 1591, at the same time as he rebuilt the Hall there. Both the Hall and its gardens were on a vast scale, as befitted a man of Hatton's position.

Another extraordinary garden is that at Lyveden New Bield in Northamptonshire. The curious incomplete structure on the hilltop, now owned by the National Trust, always impresses visitors, though it can also puzzle them. It was apparently intended to be a house, for it contains kitchens, fine apartments and bedrooms. It also has obvious religious connections, for its plan is in the form of a Cross, it is decorated with panels containing symbols of the Passion and has a long Latin dedication to Christ and the Virgin Mary carved around its eaves. It was erected in the 1590s by Sir Thomas Tresham, a noted convert to Roman Catholicism, who suffered long periods in prison as a result of his beliefs.

But what is the building? In fact it was designed as an elaborate summer house or banqueting hall, to

be set at the end of a garden to accompany a great house which was never built. Tresham began the work, but died before it was completed. Only the unfinished summer house stands, though in the woodland to the north of it the observant visitor will notice water-filled canals, great earthen mounts of double truncated pyramidal form and long embanked terraces. These are parts of the great garden, also never completed.

Tresham created other gardens at his main house, Rushton, in Northamptonshire; in the corner of the present garden, and now in the care of the State, is another of his remarkable buildings, the Triangular Lodge.

This too is really only a small summer house, but it is also a mixture of Elizabethan symbolism and an expression of Tresham's faith. As its name suggests, it is triangular in plan; it is also built in threes. There are three chimneys with three pots, three floors, three windows on each floor, each with three lights, and so on. It is a symbol of the Trinity.

When it was built in the 1580s, Holdenby House, Northamptonshire, was one of the largest country houses in England, as befitted its owner, Sir Christopher Hatton, Lord Chancellor from 1587 to 1591. It was surrounded by magnificent formal gardens. The house was pulled down in the 1650s and nothing but a few fragments survived when this engraving was made in the eighteenth century. Now only the arched gates and the terraces of the gardens remain.

Lyveden New Bield, Northamptonshire, was built in the 1590s for Sir Thomas Tresham. Intended as a garden house or banqueting hall, it was not completed before Tresham's death and was then abandoned.

All these gardens and garden features are in a sense single-period remains, in that they were laid out or built at a certain time, and then soon abandoned. They offer eloquent examples of the scenic ideals of their period.

Perhaps more interesting, because they are more typical of English life, are those gardens and parks which were constantly altered to take account of changing fashions throughout the seventeenth, eighteenth and nineteenth centuries. The great park at Wimpole – in which so many major landscape gardeners were at some time involved – has already been noted. Another, equally remarkable, is at Wrest Park, Silsoe, in Bedfordshire, now a State monument. It was begun in 1706 by the Duke of Kent, in a fashionable semi-formal manner. Of this phase, the Long Water, a magnificent long pond with a splendid domed pavilion designed by Thomas Archer at its end, as well as intersecting paths through woodland, still survives. Then, in 1740, the Second Earl of Hardwick employed Capability Brown to make the gardens less formal, in keeping with new tastes. Brown added serpentine lakes and opened up the gardens with spacious lawns. The gardens were modified again in the 1830s with the addition of a French-style section which was added to in the late nineteenth century. Other remarkable features include a Bowling Green House of 1735, designed by Batty Langley, the Orangery of 1836, and a Chinese Bridge of 1874.

These gardens and parks were, of course, carefully manipulated settings for the houses within them. Mid Anglia contains a large number of extraordinarily fine great houses which together show the development of architecture, taste and fashion over a four-hundred year period. Perhaps more importantly, they also show how people's ideas of living changed over the same period.

As we have already seen, in

As in so many parts of England, Mid Anglia bears the stamp of Capability Brown, above (1715–83). The parks at Wimpole and Madingley, in Cambridgeshire, at Fawsley, Castle Ashby, Althorp, Aynho and Wakefield Lodge, in Northamptonshire, and at Ampthill, Luton Hoo, Southill and Wrest Park, in Bedfordshire, are all basically his work.

medieval times the most important part of a major house was the Great Hall. The concept of a hall was admirably suited to the lifestyles of medieval times, for within it most of the activities of upper-class society could be carried out. Feasting, lavish entertaining, games, and even sleeping – at least by the lower members of a lordly household – could all take place there. Yet the open hall was only part of a medieval lord's home. The cooking and preparation of food required kitchens and these were usually added to the end of the hall and separated from it by an entrance passage, the latter cut off from the hall by a screen. Such medieval arrangements, with hall,

'screens passages' and kitchen beyond, still survive in many Cambridge colleges, and much altered versions may be seen at some of the great country houses, such as Deene Park in Northamptonshire.

But medieval lords, though happy to join in the feasting in the great hall, also desired private rooms. These were usually built at the opposite end of the hall to the kitchen and included parlours and bedrooms. Thus the 'normal' medieval great house consisted of a long range of buildings, made up of a central hall with kitchen area at one end and private apartments at the other. In addition, at the houses of major lords, extra rooms for servants, visitors and

Deene Park, Northamptonshire, where the medieval concept of the interior remains visible despite later changes made in the Elizabethan, Jacobean and Georgian periods.

stores were necessary and these were often arranged around a central courtyard and approached by a gateway. These medieval houses rarely had a regular layout, or anything that approached a balanced or symmetrical appearance. Windows, doors, chimneys, and so on were placed for the convenience of the inhabitants, not to impress the outside observer. Most would be described as 'rambling' rather than 'imposing'.

No medieval house remains complete in Mid Anglia so it is difficult within the region to visualize this almost-ubiquitous house form, though the late-medieval great hall at Boughton has survived together with its tiny central courtyard.

By the sixteenth century, life in the great houses of Mid Anglia was changing rapidly, as new ideas and demands for an improved standard of living, as well as new fashions in architecture, all pressed upon house builders. Yet these changes did not result in totally different houses. As always when people's homes are under discussion, new ideas were mixed up with traditional ways of living, and compromises emerged. Architectural fashion in the sixteenth century demanded elaborate external and internal decoration, usually in the new 'Renaissance' style, and a symmetry of external appearance with regularly spaced windows and central entrances. Now an 'imposing' appearance *was* the aim. In addition, greatly increased numbers of private bedrooms and living rooms for the family, servants and visitors gradually became regarded as a necessity.

Yet, at the same time, the traditional great hall (even if it was only used for great occasions) was thought to be an absolute necessity, because it was both a traditional feature and because it was a status symbol. All these demands were difficult to achieve without some compromise and it is largely because of this that sixteenth- and early seventeenth-century country houses are so interesting.

Kirby Hall, Northamptonshire. The arrangement of the hall may be medieval, but the architecture is certainly not. The house is largely decorated with Renaissance details of high quality. The surrounding gardens date from the 1680s.

Sir Christopher Hatton (1540–91), Gentleman Pensioner, Captain of the Queen's Guard, Gentleman of the Privy Chamber, Vice-Chamberlain, High Steward of the University of Cambridge, Chancellor of the University of Oxford, Knight of the Garter, Privy Counsellor, Lord High Chancellor of England, Queen Elizabeth I's favourite, and builder of Holdenby and Kirby Halls, Northamptonshire.

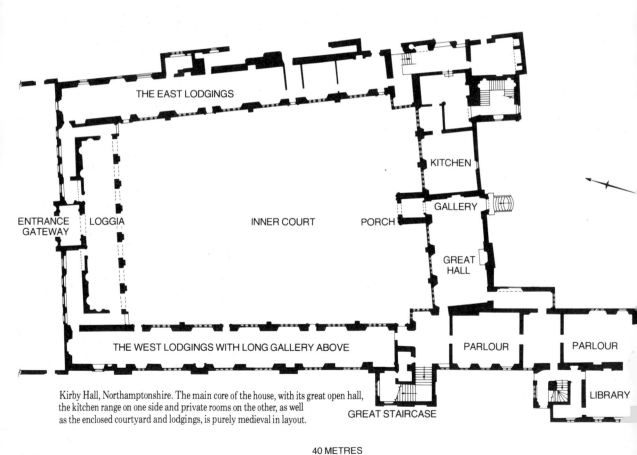

THE EAST LODGINGS

KITCHEN

ENTRANCE GATEWAY | LOGGIA

INNER COURT

PORCH

GALLERY

GREAT HALL

THE WEST LODGINGS WITH LONG GALLERY ABOVE

PARLOUR

PARLOUR

LIBRARY

GREAT STAIRCASE

Kirby Hall, Northamptonshire. The main core of the house, with its great open hall, the kitchen range on one side and private rooms on the other, as well as the enclosed courtyard and lodgings, is purely medieval in layout.

40 METRES

The problems and their solutions are best seen at Kirby Hall in Northamptonshire, begun in 1570 for Sir Humphry Stafford, a local magnate. It was bought in 1570 by Sir Christopher Hatton, a much more important person. Hatton, as was mentioned earlier in the context of Holdenby, was to become Lord Chancellor. He and his immediate descendants finished the Hall. The design of Kirby is, at first sight, an impressive example of the new ideas of Renaissance and Classical architecture. It is approached through an entrance gateway set in the centre of a symmetrical block. The inner courtyard is bounded on two sides by symmetrical 'lodgings' and on the third by an arcaded loggia with almost pure Italian decoration. The fourth side is occupied by the house itself, again exactly symmetrical with a central porch. So far all is 'modern'. But, on entering the house through the porch, the visitor is back in a medieval hall, open to the roof, with doors at one end leading to the kitchens in their traditional place, and another door at the other end leading to the private apartments. Suddenly all is clear. The symmetry of the front of the house and its porch has been achieved by pushing the hall to one side of the building and cleverly disguising the kitchen block which forms the other half with matching windows and columns. Here is the compromise between the old way of life and the new architecture.

Another version of this compromise can be seen at Burghley House, near Stamford. This was built by an even greater man than Hatton, William Cecil, First Lord Burghley and Lord High Treasurer to Elizabeth I between 1556 and 1589. Externally it is almost pure Classical Renaissance in style with elaborately symmetrical elevations and perhaps the most remarkable skyline of any English country house, its towers, turrets and immensely tall chimneys apparently scattered in random profusion but actually carefully regimented.

Burghley House, Cambridgeshire, set magnificently in a parkland two hundred years younger than itself. The house shows well the aims and desires of the greatest of the Elizabethan statesmen.

William Cecil (1520–98), Lord Burghley, Lord High Treasurer of England, arguably the most important, powerful and influential man of Queen Elizabeth I's reign. He built Burghley House over a long period, between 1552 and 1587, and it has been the home of the Cecils ever since.

Most of the interior of the house has been altered and belongs to another age. Yet it still has its original great open hall in the medieval tradition. And here the massive timber double hammerbeam roof of pure late medieval type has Renaissance pendants, and the huge fireplace is entirely Classical in design.

Houses built by lesser men often had much less 'modern' architecture with much more of the medieval tradition preserved. One such is Canons Ashby in Northamptonshire, built in the 1550s for the Dryden family. It still retains its enclosed courtyard, and though decorated in a sub-Classical style it is decidedly 'old-fashioned' in its overall appearance when compared with houses such as Kirby and Burghley. It too has its great hall, once open to the roof, but now with a low inserted ceiling. This latter is an important and recurring feature from the late sixteenth century onwards, when the tradition of a great hall became less fashionable. Certainly a hall was still required for great occasions, but more intimate and certainly warmer conditions were sought. In addition, with the changes in the way that people conducted their private lives, extra rooms were at a premium. Thus, by inserting a ceiling into the hall which formerly had been open to the roof, the owner acquired a more satisfactory hall and could install new bedrooms in the space above it.

Canons Ashby, Northamptonshire, before restoration by the National Trust. The west side, rebuilt in 1708–10, reveals how the owners tried to fit an early eighteenth-century façade on a sixteenth-century framework which included a great tower.

Many late sixteenth- and early seventeenth-century houses were built with halls already reduced in this fashion. A particularly good example, not least because it indicates the way of life of the upper classes at this time, is Madingley Hall, near Cambridge. It was built by the Hyndes, a family of wealthy lawyers, between 1547 and 1590. On the ground floor is a hall, with its traditional screens passage and kitchen range beyond. But above it is another hall. This was remodelled to form a 'saloon' in the early eighteenth century, but originally it was a huge hall open to the roof which was supported by a false hammerbeam construction. Here we have the curious presence of two halls in the same house, yet all is explicable in terms of the social life of the day. The lower hall was the place for traditional social occasions while the upper hall was the room for the family's private activities – yet it remained a hall in the medieval sense.

Other broadly contemporary houses in Mid Anglia also exhibit this long-lasting love

Madingley Hall, Cambridgeshire. Built in the late sixteenth century for the Hynde family, the house is both old-fashioned in arrangement yet up-to-date in appearance.

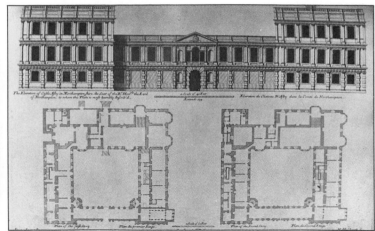

Above: Inigo Jones, architect (1573–1652), possibly the designer of the courtyard screen at Castle Ashby and the porch at Kirby Hall. Certainly he was responsible for the Stoke Park Pavilions, Northamptonshire.

Above right and below: Castle Ashby, Northamptonshire. Begun by the First Lord Compton in 1574, it was not completed until well into the seventeenth century. It is a typical Elizabethan and Jacobean house both in its symmetrical appearance and overall plan.

affair with the hall. Their halls often still survive despite many alterations and additions. A small hall forms the core of the old part of the house at Rockingham Castle, while that at Castle Ashby, begun by the First Lord Compton in 1574, originally formed one range of a three-sided block. The fourth side of this square was added slightly later to produce an enclosed courtyard. Castle Ashby House illustrates another important aspect of the great houses of this period. The ground floor is a loggia, open to the court with, above, a long gallery decorated with Classical details that suggest the work of the great early seventeenth-century architect Inigo Jones.

Long galleries made an important contribution as 'places for living'. In the late sixteenth century and early seventeenth century no house of distinction could afford to be without a long gallery which, once decorated with pictures and hangings, provided an intimate area for exercise on wet days, as well as a place for social gatherings. The position of the long gallery at Castle Ashby, enclosing

the formerly open courtyard, fitted in well with the existing house. Elsewhere, the siting of a long gallery could cause problems, for the necessarily elongated structure might easily destroy the external symmetry of a building. At Kirby Hall the difficulty was solved by using the first floor of one of the ranges of lodgings around the courtyard as a gallery. At Madingley, there was no convenient courtyard to enclose or range of buildings to adapt. The long gallery, set above an open loggia, had to be built as a projecting wing and this wrecked the otherwise symmetrical elevation. Although this wing has now been pulled down, its later and shorter replacement still illustrates well the difficulties of combining external visual aims with internal household requirements in the sixteenth and early seventeenth centuries.

The mid seventeenth century saw the arrival in Mid Anglia of a very different form of great house. The conditions which brought it into being were exactly the same as those in the previous period, a desire for external symmetry and more complex and different living conditions within, but now these ideals were taken to their logical conclusion. Internally, the great hall lost its ancient function and became little more than a vestibule or entrance compartment around which were set a whole host of other rooms with specialized functions, such as dining rooms, salons, drawing rooms, and so on. As the kitchens no longer needed to be next to the hall, they could be placed well away from it, either at the rear of the house or even in the basement. The reduced status of the hall and its central relationship to the surrounding rooms enabled external symmetry to be achieved more easily, with the main entrance set in the centre of the elevation and all windows and applied decorations arranged neatly on either side.

Wimpole Hall shows this feature admirably as well as displaying later developments. The earliest part of the house was built by Sir Thomas Chicheley about 1640. The exterior of the front of the house is not original, for it was refaced in the mid eighteenth century, though still with the same symmetrical form. But inside, albeit altered in detail, the original mid seventeenth-century arrangement of rooms set around a central hall survives.

Once established, this type of country house became standard for two hundred years. The numerous small late-Georgian houses in Mid Anglia, of which few are open to the public, generally conform to this pattern, both internally and externally, despite changes in architectural fashion or interior decoration.

The development of country houses did not end in the mid seventeenth century. Houses that were particularly important, or rather owned by important families, were enlarged and rebuilt, and of course many of the older houses already described were radically altered.

One important facet of fashionable society in the seventeenth and eighteenth centuries was the desire for a set of 'state rooms' which could be used by important visitors and which would also interconnect directly with each other without recourse to long passages. This was

Wimpole Hall, Cambridgeshire, one of the great houses of Mid Anglia. Although at first sight it seems all of one period, like so many English country houses it is the result of centuries of adaptation to changing living conditions.

thought necessary for two reasons. Firstly, visitors could pass through various ante-rooms on their way to meet their host, stopping for refreshment or conversation on their way. Secondly, at great parties or festive occasions, guests could gradually move round the house in a circular fashion, talking, being entertained, or eating as they went. The impact of these ideas on the interiors of the larger houses was considerable. Again Wimpole stands out as a remarkable example. When the wings on either side of the original house were added in the late seventeenth and early eighteenth centuries, the west wing was designed with this circulating pattern in mind. The present way that visitors to Wimpole move round the ground floor is very much as was intended for guests in the eighteenth century, who passed from entrance hall to ante-room to drawing room, gallery, dining room and so on.

Many of the older houses of the area are adapted to have the same arrangement of rooms with the same pattern of circulation and all were decorated to the height of fashion. At Burghley, the state rooms are on the first floor, all elaborately painted and fitted into one of the long sides of the original house. The same pattern occurs at Castle Ashby. At Boughton, the First Duke of Montagu, who had been ambassador to the French court in the 1670s, added a huge north front in a totally French style in the 1680s.

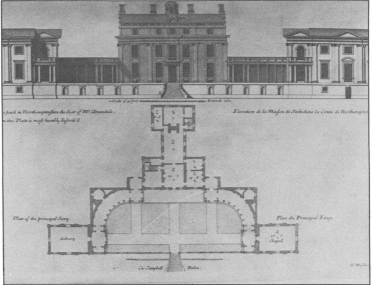

This contained a range of state rooms, again with elaborately painted ceilings.

Of course, these state rooms were only used on great occasions, and the families who lived there usually had much less elaborate and much more intimate suites of rooms elsewhere in the house. However, most of the great houses

Top: When it was erected in 1629–30, Stoke Park was probably the most unusual house in England, built to Italian designs then virtually unknown in this country. It soon became the model for many later houses. The house itself no longer exists, but the side pavilions still stand.
Above: Kelmarsh Hall, Northamptonshire. This view shows the old Elizabethan house at Kelmarsh, replaced by the present one in 1727–32.

were conceived as places of entertainment as much as, if not more than, homes, and the arrangement of their rooms reflects this system of priorities.

Lower down the social scale, the small country houses were much less elaborate and were intended to function more truly as family homes. Perhaps the best example is Hinwick House in Bedfordshire, built in a delightful Queen Anne style between 1709 and 1714. It has no great state rooms, or lavish entertainment areas. The main entrance door opens directly into a spacious hall which leads to a large staircase hall and other family rooms set on either side.

As the eighteenth century advanced, a number of houses were either built with, or altered to have, flanking pavilions. These were usually linked to the main house by curving passages or colonnaded verandahs. The original design was late sixteenth-century Italian, and the earliest house in England of this type is at Stoke Park, Northamptonshire, built in 1629–36. The house itself no longer

exists, but the colonnades and pavilions still stand. This arrangement was copied again and again in the eighteenth century, as at Kelmarsh Hall (1727–32), Biggin Hall (where the pavilions were added about 1750) and Cottesbrook (the pavilions being added about 1770 to an older house of 1702–13), all in Northamptonshire. A much humbler example is Little Shelford Manor House, Cambridgeshire, of about 1750.

Alongside these traditional developments there was always a crop of curious and eccentric houses. Kimbolton Castle, Cambridgeshire, built by the architect Vanbrugh for the Fourth Duke of Manchester between 1707 and 1714, is one such example. Like so many other houses it was not built anew but around and incorporating a much older Tudor house arranged round a courtyard. Thus in some respects it is strangely old-fashioned, despite the Classical columns and portico on the main front. For behind the entrance is a great hall – decorated, it is true, in a purely eighteenth-century way –

which is actually the original Tudor hall.

Far more unusual and of a much later date is Wrest Park. The original Jacobean house was pulled down and replaced in 1834–36 by a totally French building designed by a French architect, Clephane. It was unique in England when it was built, and it still stands rather oddly in the Bedfordshire countryside.

By this time, the concept of country houses had changed yet again. The different demands of upper-class society were forcing the architects to produce houses with a vast array of special rooms for family living, house parties and great occasions. Smoking rooms, billiard rooms, parlours, drawing rooms, breakfast rooms were all needed as well as nurseries for the enlarged families and, in particular, working and living accommodation for huge numbers of servants. Such demands could hardly fit into the standard arrangement of the earlier houses without massive alterations or rebuilding which would destroy the external symmetry of the previous

Kimbolton Castle, Cambridgeshire. It was rebuilt in 1707–14 by Vanbrugh to a deliberately severe design intended to produce a 'masculine' character.

period. Symmetry, however, was going out of fashion, and being replaced by an asymmetrical Gothic style that favoured towers, wings, gables and so on – features which were admirably suited to the assorted rooms behind. Thus emerged the Victorian country house in all its glory.

Mid Anglia does not have a great number of examples, but the Gothic Milton Ernest Hall in Bedfordshire, built in 1856, demonstrates the demands and the solutions admirably, while Maidwell Hall, Northamptonshire (1885), in a Jacobean style, is a little less flamboyant. The most curious is Overstone Hall, Northamptonshire (1860), built for the First Lord Overstone, a rich Victorian banker. It has almost every known European architectural style somewhere in its walls and no architectural historian has ever been able to describe its details.

Many of the older country houses were, of course, enlarged and altered in Victorian times. The most successful conversions involved the large medieval and sixteenth- to early seventeenth-century houses, whose ranges of rooms could be changed and added to with comparative ease. Thus at Deene Park, a Tudoresque range was added to the older house in 1830 and a gigantic ballroom (since removed) attached in 1865. Wimpole Hall also had very large and not entirely pleasing wings added to it in the 1840s, and we should perhaps be thankful that these too have been taken down. Another house which was changed almost out of all recognition in the nineteenth century and later is Luton Hoo in Bedfordshire. The original house was begun by Robert Adam in 1764 and altered by Robert Smirke about 1827. But a disastrous fire in 1843 and some indifferent alterations left it as an undistinguished house until 1903, when the interior was remodelled for Sir Julius Wernher, a South African diamond magnate. The work was done by the architects who had also

designed the Ritz and Waldorf Hotels in London. The result is a house sumptuously decorated in a magnificent combination of late nineteenth-century French and English Edwardian splendour. The important Wernher art collection now housed within it should not blind the visitor to the setting, which is in a class by itself.

The changed circumstances of the twentieth century have meant the end of country house building, and many existing houses have been demolished or shorn of additions. Only one recent house is really worthy of note, Ashby St Ledgers in Northamptonshire, and that is really a rebuilding of an older house, much of which still remains.

Top left: Robert Adam, architect (1728–92). Adam built Luton Hoo, in Bedfordshire, though little of his work remains, and designed the gate house at Kimbolton, Cambridgeshire.
Top right and above: Externally Luton Hoo, Bedfordshire, is a fairly undistinguished building. Inside, however, as a result of its redecoration in 1903, it is one of the most notable houses of its period in Britain. **Top:** Marble Hall. **Above:** Dining Room.

Designed by Sir Edwin Lutyens for the Second Lord Wimborne, it is a delightful mixture of genuine sixteenth- and seventeenth-century work in stone, with stone and timber-framed ranges added by Lutyens to produce an informal arrangement that merges with its surroundings in a truly English way.

Less successful is Anglesey Abbey in Cambridgeshire, owned by the National Trust. Here Lord Fairhaven tried to turn a rather undistinguished minor house into a gentleman's residence. The attempt was not exactly a triumph and Anglesey remains something of a curiosity amongst the country houses of the area. On the other hand the gardens at Anglesey are remarkable and show what can be achieved on a site which is so unprepossessing that most landscape gardeners and designers would have given up. Lord Fairhaven did not, and the result is a splendidly informal yet formalized park-like garden.

Sir Edwin Lutyens (1869–1944), perhaps the greatest English architect of the last hundred years. Lutyens designed cottages, houses, mansions, The Cenotaph, and the new Indian capital at Delhi. His alterations to Ashby St Ledgers House, Northamptonshire, are little known but are typical of his work.

Anglesey Abbey, Cambridgeshire. This small, undistinguished seventeenth-century country house, built on the ruins of a medieval monastery, was enlarged and altered by Lord Fairhaven between 1926 and 1958.

The 'Great Rebuilding'

Just as the country houses of Mid Anglia reflect the development of upper-class taste and living over the last four hundred years, so the smaller houses demonstrate the styles of their owners. With very few exceptions most of the 'period' houses and cottages in Mid Anglia are of late sixteenth-century or more recent date. Few medieval houses of the ordinary people survive, at least in a form that we can easily recognize. This is because in the late sixteenth and early seventeenth centuries, in our region as elsewhere, massive numbers of new houses were built by all but the very poor, so much so that this phase has been termed the 'Great Rebuilding'.

The causes of so much rebuilding are complex and relate to increasing wealth at all levels of society, new ideas and higher living standards. Even so, in the late sixteenth and early seventeenth centuries, the new houses were strictly conditioned by the limits of contemporary building technology, as well as by what was thought to be the 'ideal', indeed traditional, way of living. Most farmhouses and cottages and even small manor houses were single-range buildings only one room deep, and consisted of a heated living room with a fireplace, perhaps another heated room and a third unheated room on the ground floor, with bedrooms above. The main room was the living room, often termed a hall as the direct descendant of the medieval halls that were designed for communal living. If extra rooms were needed, other ranges were merely added to provide L-shaped, T-shaped or even U-shaped house plans. The external appearances of such houses did not matter so much. They might have been built of stone, timber, or indeed of mud. Their roofs might be thatched, tiled, or have stone 'slates'. But the arrangement of doors and windows was conditioned by the arrangement of rooms within them. They did not join the quest for external symmetry.

As we have seen, at the higher levels of society symmetrical elevations arrived in the sixteenth century and most country houses conformed to this new architectural aim. Lower down the social scale it was some time before such ideas were accepted. It was not until the late seventeenth century that we find a few of the better-class farmhouses and small manor houses with symmetrical fronts, and many of these are merely façades. Docwra's Manor at Shepreth, in Cambridgeshire, is a splendid example. When viewed from the front through its eighteenth-century iron gates, it appears to be a fine early eighteenth-century house of red brick, with blue brick trimmings, a symmetrical elevation and central door surrounded by attached Tuscan columns with a delightful Venetian window above. Yet viewed from the side, the observant visitor sees that this front is only one brick thick and literally stuck on to an L-shaped seventeenth-century timber-framed house.

Docwra's Manor also exhibits another stage in the changes made to houses at this time. We saw earlier that in the seventeenth century large country houses developed a double-depth plan with rooms set

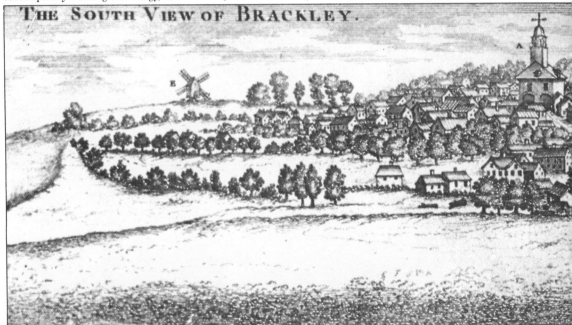

Despite its inevitable expansion in modern times Brackley, Northamptonshire, remains today, as it was in the eighteenth century, a delightful small country town, one of the best in England.

round an entrance hall. At Docwra's Manor we can see this development taking place. The seventeenth-century house with its new front must have looked modern and acceptable to passers-by in the 1720s, but inside it was still L-shaped and had, by then, awkward and old-fashioned room arrangements. So a few years later the space within the 'L' was filled in, producing a double-depth building and allowing the formation of a central entrance hall with a staircase beyond, and with dining and drawing rooms on either side.

This fashion for symmetry both inside and out soon spread all over rural Mid Anglia. By the end of the eighteenth century all new farmhouses, rectories, manor houses and even modest cottages had symmetrical fronts and, usually, central entrance halls. During the nineteenth century almost all new houses, even the smallest cottages, had such a plan and appearance, though the latter were often built without an entrance hall so that the front door opened directly into the living room. All this took place almost regardless of building materials. Stone was still used in the traditional stone areas and rendered dried mud blocks were used in the east until well into the nineteenth century. Then, first local bricks and then the ubiquitous 'Flettons' from Peterborough displaced the traditional materials, while Welsh slates pushed out clay or stone tiles and thatch.

Most of the towns of Mid Anglia prospered and grew rich in the seventeenth and eighteenth centuries. Yet, such is the nature of towns, if they prosper little of their earlier prosperity tends to survive, but is removed to make way for a later phase of urban progress and its accompanying expressions of wealth or status. Neither Bedford nor Northampton has many buildings dating from before the nineteenth century, and in Northampton a fire in the seventeenth century aided the general destruction. Cambridge removed most of its old buildings, apart from the University and Colleges, during the last hundred years, and the same is true at Peterborough and Luton in more recent times.

It is the smaller towns, places which reached their greatest prosperity in the eighteenth and nineteenth centuries, and which now either remain as local market centres or have had some protection against large-scale modern redevelopment, that we have to visit to see what most towns must have looked like two hundred years ago, when they were often small islands of provincial urban culture set in totally rural surroundings. Most are characterized by town centres based on market squares of different sizes and often edged by pretty eighteenth- and nineteenth-century town houses.

The best example is Brackley in Northamptonshire, not because its Georgian architecture is particularly fine, but because of its setting. The broad market place, punctuated by the splendid Town Hall of 1706, and lined by brick and some stone houses and shops, must surely be one of the finest townscapes in England. By comparison, the great market place at St Neots, Cambridgeshire, though impressive in scale and containing a number of pleasant Georgian brick buildings, is dull. Higham Ferrers,

A. The Town Hall. B. The College. C. St ...

Above: North Brink, Wisbech, Cambridgeshire. Here, set on the side of the River Nene and away from the commercial bustle of the town centre are the houses of the great merchants and bankers who prospered in the eighteenth and nineteenth centuries when Wisbech was a major port. North Brink has been described as 'one of the most perfect Georgian streets of England.'
Right: Peckover House, North Brink, Wisbech, Cambridgeshire. Built in the 1720s for the Peckovers, a banking family, the house is the finest building in the town.

Northamptonshire, with its small triangular market place and uniformly stone-built houses, is much more attractive, despite the modern through road. Architecturally the best town is Ampthill in Bedfordshire, where, particularly in Church Street, there are a number of extremely fine eighteenth-century houses. Towcester, Daventry and Huntingdon all have many fine eighteenth-century buildings in their centres, while the little-known Potton, in Bedfordshire, with its red-brick eighteenth-century houses set around a small square, is especially worthy of note.

Wisbech, since medieval times a sea port, is also notable for its eighteenth- and nineteenth-century architecture, the best examples being the houses of the rich merchants and businessmen set along the North Brink on the edge of the River Nene. Of these the finest by far is Peckover House, now a National Trust property.

After the Reformation, few churches in Mid Anglia were rebuilt. In the majority of cases, at most a mere restoration of the medieval structures was undertaken. The churches that were totally reconstructed were not only built in a new style, they were also planned to take account of the post-Reformation liturgical demands. The best is All Saints, Northampton, rebuilt after a fire in 1676 – 80 in a style which is so remarkable that it outshines almost anything outside London. At a lesser level, Stoke Doyle Church (1727), in Northamptonshire, and the tower of Leighton Bromswold (1634), in Cambridgeshire, are particularly interesting, though the gem of the region must be Little Gidding Church (1714), also in Cambridgeshire, not least because of its religious associations with the de Ferrers family.

Restoration of churches went on apace in Victorian times and many were enlarged or extended. One of the most remarkable of all recent churches is St Mary's, Wellingborough, Northamptonshire, designed by Sir Ninian Comper and built between 1908 and 1930 in a glorious mixture of styles which somehow succeed in forming an amazing unity.

Roads, Canals and Railways

The last three hundred years have seen a revolution in methods of transport. During the medieval period roads were ill-kept tracks, and difficult to move along. Only the bridges of those times were carefully and often elaborately constructed as a result of bequests by lords and clerics. Mid Anglia has a wealth of fine medieval bridges, including those across the River Ouse at Huntingdon and St Ives in Cambridgeshire, Great Barford, Harrold and Bromham in Bedfordshire, and Thrapston, across the River Nene, in Northamptonshire. A rare survival, itself redolent of medieval methods of transport, is the tiny pack-horse bridge at Charwelton in Northamptonshire.

From the late seventeenth century onwards, roads were greatly improved, resulting in a considerable increase in traffic, especially wheeled vehicles, and this work continued into the early nineteenth century with the age of coaching. Great inns such as The George at Huntingdon and The Haycock at Wansford, Cambridgeshire, appeared, and milestones and direction signs proliferated. The earliest milestones in England, apart from the Roman examples, were erected in 1725–32 and still remain on the old London Road out of Cambridge via Trumpington, Harston, Newton and Fowlmere. These were provided by money left to Trinity Hall,

Despite being on a modern main trunk road, the tiny medieval pack-horse bridge across the infant River Cherwell at Charwelton, Northamptonshire, still remains inviolate as it did when this photograph was taken around 1900.

Milestone, Newton, Cambridgeshire: one of a group of milestones on the old London road from Cambridge, built between 1725 and 1732.

Cambridge, in 1552 by Dr William Mowse, the then Master. Hence they are decorated with the arms of Mowse and the College. Other more elaborate direction posts include the block surmounted by a finial in the centre of the A1 at Alconbury Hill and the triangular obelisk at Brampton, Cambridgeshire, both of the eighteenth century. The new roads also needed new bridges, now designed by engineer/architects. Many are graceful structures, often quite unnoticed by the travellers who cross them, though that at Bedford, built in 1811–13, can be viewed with advantage from the river walks and embankment near it. Others, such as the splendid one built in 1815–20 across the River Ouse at Tempsford, Bedfordshire, can only be appreciated

Direction obelisk, Brampton, Cambridgeshire. Although the road junction on which it stands has now been bypassed, its position marks the meeting place of two major eighteenth-century roads.

by those lucky enough to use the river.

From the late seventeenth century many major roads were 'turnpiked' and travellers paid their way at various toll houses, a few of which survive including those at Trumpington and Barnwell on the outskirts of Cambridge. Most turnpike roads were old routes with improved surfaces, though some were subjected to major improvements and re-alignments. The most notable of these is the present A5 between Old Stratford and Weedon in Northamptonshire. Its long straight alignments derive from its origin as the Roman road Watling Street. But the Roman engineers built it rising and falling over a succession of steep hills and deep valleys and the medieval traveller saw no reason to change this. In the 1820s, however, it became part of the London – Holyhead main road and was almost totally rebuilt by Thomas Telford. Telford widened the old road, cut through the ridge tops and filled in the valleys with embankments and put in sweeping curves. Travellers speeding along that section of the A5 today owe more to Telford's work than that of the Roman builders.

The late eighteenth century brought a new form of transport to part of Mid Anglia: canals. The most notable was the Grand Junction (now the Grand Union) Canal, which traverses Northamptonshire. Its line is punctuated by neat lock-keepers' houses and graceful bridges, including an elaborately decorated stone structure at Cosgrove and a splendid cast-iron one at Braunston. More exciting are the great tunnels at Braunston and Blisworth. At the south end of the latter is Stoke Bruerne which, with its locks, barges, pub and warehouse (now a waterway museum), encapsulates the spirit of the canal era.

On the eastern fens, waterborne traffic was important even in Roman times, and in the medieval period most fen-edge villages were minor ports. Dock Lane, in Horningsea, and The Hythe, in Fen Ditton, are both names given to streets leading to former riverside wharves, while at Reach, also in Cambridgeshire, the huge village green and The Hythe are all part of a small medieval port linked to the River Cam by a three-mile canal. The nearby hamlet of Commercial End, with its merchant's house, warehouses and neat rows of cottages was largely rebuilt in the 1820s by a water transport firm that controlled trade in the area.

This fenland trade, conducted via canal and road, lost its importance after 1840 with the coming of the railways, which changed not only the landscape but the habits of the nation. Until the Beeching cuts of the 1960s, Mid Anglia was criss-crossed by railways serving tiny communities and great towns alike. Now all but the main lines have gone. Yet much of interest remains. The remarkable station at Cambridge, largely unaltered, is unique in Britain, with its single platform and central crossing. Strangely Gothic or Tudoresque station houses can still be recognized in what seem to be the most unlikely places, having been left stranded when the trains and the track vanished for ever.

One of the odder remnants of the railway age is at Woodford Halse, Northamptonshire. The village, with its stone and thatched cottages and small church, seems a totally rural place. Then suddenly one finds rows of neat red-brick terraces seemingly straight from a late nineteenth-century town. These were built in 1896, when the main line of the Great Central Railway was cut across the area, to house the workers in the adjacent sidings and locomotive depot. Now only the houses and the gigantic empty cuttings are left. Woodford, after a brief flirtation with the outside world, has returned to its rural slumber.

Horningsea, Cambridgeshire. In late Saxon times the church was a minster, and may have been situated at the centre of a great estate. In the medieval period the proximity of the River Cam led to the village becoming a small inland port.

Reach Lode, Cambridgeshire, constructed originally as a canal by the Romans. It was re-cut and used in medieval times to link the navigable River Cam to the fen-edge port of Reach. Its life was ended by the coming of the railways and it is now only used by the occasional river cruiser.

Apart from the carriages and costumes, Cambridge Station has changed but little since it was opened in 1845. It remains unique both in its appearance and in its train-working methods.

The Twentieth Century

Perhaps we are still too close to the events of the last eighty years or so to see them objectively or assess their impact on the landscape of Mid Anglia. The region has certainly escaped the worst excesses of large-scale planning and industrial development, although Cambridgeshire has been devastated by modern agriculture. Only Peterborough and Luton can be considered major industrial towns, and even there most of the larger factories are out of sight of the town centres. Only the towering chimneys of the London Brick Company's works at Peterborough, whose great clay pits lie below them, are an obvious intrusion into the scene, as are the similar brick works south-west of Bedford. The latter have given rise to a fascinating new village, Stewartby, especially laid out in 1927.

Between the medieval period and the beginning of this century, Mid Anglia was little involved in either the preparations for war or its actuality. The one major exception was the Civil War of the mid

Brick-working is the only major extractive industry in Mid Anglia. The tall chimneys of Stewartby may disfigure the Bedfordshire landscape, but from them have poured the millions of bricks that form many of our homes.

seventeenth century when the area was subjected to numerous sieges and attacks by both sides. Vast numbers of gun batteries and siegeworks were constructed, but all were temporary and few have survived later activities. The most interesting, and certainly one of the best Civil War forts in Britain, is that known as The Bulwarks. It lies just north of the Huntingdon–Ely road between the Old and New Bedford Rivers at Earith in Cambridgeshire. Here the earthen ramparts of great 'angle bastions', built to take heavy cannon, and the surrounding ditch emplacements for musketeers, all survive.

A military curiosity of the Napoleonic Wars is Weedon Barracks, near Northampton. When invasion was threatened in 1803 it was decided to build a barracks, store houses and a refuge for King George III at a point in the country furthest from the sea. The barracks were sited not only at a major road junction, but also beside the recently built Grand Junction Canal. A spur from the canal was constructed into the barracks and a great wharf, lined by store houses, was created, and protected by a gate house with a portcullis which blocked

The Bulwarks, Earith, Cambridgeshire. The finest seventeenth-century Civil War fort in England. The main fort with its four great bastions projecting from a square ramparted core is of standard design. The long outworks extending across the fields on two sides are unique.

Weedon Barracks, Northamptonshire, in the early nineteenth century. Set in the centre of England and linked to both road and canal, it was intended to be a place of last resort in the event of a Napoleonic invasion. The great 'palace' built for George III has gone, but the barracks and canal wharfs remain.

the canal spur. The whole arrangement now seems an odd military concept, though the site remained a defence establishment until only a few years ago.

Two World Wars and the threat of a third have left the region littered with abandoned and still-functioning military establishments. Some of these are of considerable historical interest, and even aesthetically pleasing. At Cardington, south of Bedford, the landscape is dominated by two mighty airship hangars. One was built in 1917 and then enlarged, and in 1927 given its neighbour to house the ill-fated R101 and the R100. They are only part of a large industrial complex started in 1917 by the aircraft firm of Short Brothers. Amongst the other buildings of interest are a number of early workshops and a gigantic administrative building in a sub-Classical style, and a garden village for the workers called Shortstown.

The First World War has also left its mark at the early military airfield of Duxford, Cambridgeshire, now part of the Imperial War Museum. The two hangars which survive, as well as some other minor buildings, date from 1917. Most of the other buildings relate to a greater period in RAF Duxford's history: the Battle of Britain when Douglas Bader's squadron was based here. The Neo-Georgian HQ buildings, Officers' Mess and Barrack Blocks were all erected in 1935–37 ready for the station to become a Sector Airfield controlling the southern part of 12 Group, Fighter Command, during the dark days of 1940. RAF Henlow, Bedfordshire, has buildings of the same immediate pre-war period, though with a less distinguished service record. It was a training station, and many thousands of National Servicemen passed through its gates.

Otherwise most of the wartime airfields of Mid Anglia are now in ruins or have disappeared. The memorial to the fallen of the US Eighth Air Force, at the site of the old Grafton Underwood Airfield in Northamptonshire and, even more poignant, the American Cemetery at Madingley, Cambridgeshire, remind us of the sacrifice of our American allies in the great conflict.

Yet we still prepare for war. The surrealist Stonehenge-like structure at RAF Chicksands, in Bedfordshire, reminds us of the ultimate weapons in the arsenal of man.

But the greatest modern impact on the landscape of Mid Anglia is not man at war, nor even at leisure, but man as an economic animal. In the drive to produce more and more food, or farming income, regardless of cost, and whether necessary or not, an agricultural revolution has taken place in the last thirty years, alongside which all other advances in agriculture and technology pale into insignificance. Thousands of miles of hedges have been ripped out or bulldozed flat. Trees and copses have been removed and carefully managed woods abandoned to impenetrable undergrowth and rotting timber. Western and southern Cambridgeshire have suffered particularly in this campaign for increased agricultural yields, with much of the good old countryside becoming little more than a dull rolling prairie-like landscape. From our present viewpoint, the twentieth century seems to be leaving little to pass on to the future in terms of cultural heritage – and this is in sharp contrast to the actions of our forefathers.

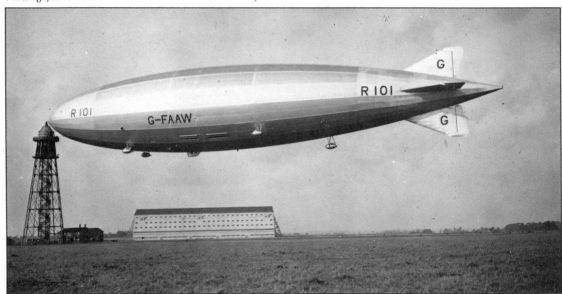

In this 1929 photograph the ill-fated R-101 seems to dwarf the hangar which housed it. In fact the airship fitted comfortably in the building, at Cardington, Bedfordshire.

A B-17 bomber preserved at the Imperial War Museum, Duxford, Cambridgeshire. The plane, the other aircraft there and indeed the airfield itself are a poignant reminder of the men of many nations who flew from the airfields of Mid Anglia in the Second World War, and of their sacrifice.

ACKNOWLEDGMENTS

The publishers are grateful to Richard Muir who took most of the photographs. Other illustrations were kindly provided by:

Aerofilms Ltd 47, top; 71 top.

BBC Hulton Picture Library 90.

Cambridgeshire Collection 40 bottom, *The North-East View of Camp's Castle,*drawn and engraved by S & N Buck, 1730; 52 bottom; 53, *Cambridge in 1574,* engraved by Richard Lyne; 56, *Conington Fen Drainage Mill 1853,* from an original by J. M. Heathcote (1800–90); 57, photo A. L. Smith & Co, March, 1900; 58 top left, top right, bottom; 59 bottom, photo 0. Ambrose; 65 bottom, *Wimpole in the County of Cambridge,* drawn by L. Knyff, engraved by I Kip; 87 bottom.

Cambridge University Collection of Air Photographs 14 both; 89 top.

Mansell Collection 55 top right, attributed to Van Mierevelt; 60 top, by E. Sariven after W. Hilton; 65 top, by J. Thompson after Sir Thomas Lawrence; 68; 78 top left.

Merton College, Oxford 31 top.

National Monuments Record 72.

National Portrait Gallery 55 top left, by Kneller; 70 top right; 79 top, by R. Lutyens.

Northamptonshire County Record Office 39 top, *Dorman's Bridges* Vol II, p 334; 48 top, *Dorman's Bridges* Vol II, p 179; 66, *Dorman's Bridges* Vol I, p 525; 74 top right, *Dorman's Bridges* Vol I, p 341; 76 both, *Dorman's Bridges* Vol I, p 328, & Vol II, p 40; 80, *History of Antiquities of Northamptonshire* (1791), p 150; 84 top; 89 bottom, *Dorman's Bridges* Vol I, p 258.

Woodmansterne Ltd 71 bottom, *William Cecil, Lord Burghley,* Bodleian Library, Oxford; 74 top left, *Inigo Jones* by W. Dobson, National Maritime Museum, Greenwich; 78 top right and bottom.

Diagrams on pages 18, 19, 25 and 70 by Bernard Thomason. Diagram on page 62 by Stephen Gyapay.

FURTHER READING

Because of its proximity to the University of Cambridge, and also because of recent exhaustive surveys by the Royal Commission on Historical Monuments, Mid Anglia is more thoroughly researched and described than almost any other region of Britain. Space does not allow us to provide a comprehensive survey of the relevant literature, but readers who would like to learn more about the history of Mid Anglia and its localities should find the following titles most helpful:

Bigmore, P. **The Bedfordshire and Huntingdonshire Landscape** (1979). This is a useful landscape history of two somewhat different counties.

Brown, D.M., Darby, C.H. and Taylor, A. **Early Cambridgeshire** (1977). Here in one volume are four smaller books which trace the history of the county from prehistoric to medieval times.

Darby, H.C. **The Changing Fenland** (1983). This is an extremely authoritative and readable account of the evolution of the Fenland landscape.

Godber, J. **History of Bedfordshire** (1969). For information on Bedfordshire, this is a thorough history of the county.

Pevsner, N. **Cambridgeshire** (2nd ed., 1970), **Huntingdonshire and Bedfordshire** (1968) and **Northamptonshire** (2nd ed., 1973). These three volumes in the **Buildings of England** series include brief descriptions of the more notable buildings of the various counties and are useful and accessible reference books.

Ravensdale, J.R. **Liable to Floods** (1974). The author of **Cornwall** in the present National Trust Series has here written a fascinating account of the history of a group of Fen-edge villages.

Ravensdale, J.R. and Muir, R. **East Anglian Landscapes** (1984). In this landscape history of East Anglia, the authors include Cambridgeshire.

Royal Commission on Historical Monuments (England) **Huntingdonshire** (1926), **City of Cambridge** (1959), **West Cambridgeshire** (1968), **N.E. Cambridgeshire** (1972) and **Northamptonshire,** Vols I–V (1975–84). These volumes provide a reasonably detailed account of the buildings, earthworks and archaeological sites of the areas concerned and should be consulted by any readers searching for more detailed insights into the antiquities and histories of particular localities.

Steane, J. **The Northamptonshire Landscape** (1974), and Taylor, C.C. **The Cambridgeshire Landscape** (1973). These are two relevant volumes from the **Making of the English Landscape** series, ed. W.G. Hoskins.

Taylor, C.C. **Village and Farmstead** (1983). This book includes many examples drawn from Mid Anglia.

Maps Also recommended for the explorer on the ground are the Ordnance Survey's Landranger (1:50,000) or Pathfinder (1:25,000) maps.

INDEX

Page numbers in italics refer to illustrations.